GW00383499

CHAPTER I

CHAPTER ONE

Early Days

Jim was born on Weymouth sea-front in early July 1941.

Well that is what his mum told him and he never knew her to tell a lie.

I am not sure the same can be said about Jim, so some of the following may be either the product of an over-active imagination or of a memory dimmed by the passing of the years, or possibly a bit of both.

Jim's birth on a seaside esplanade during wartime may not be your idea of a promising start to his life but he tells me that it wasn't quite like that. Rather that his mum, Florrie, was in a bed in a 'Nursing Home' situated amongst the sea-front hotels.

Home births were usual at this time so why she went into the Nursing Home is not known and was something Jim never asked her about. Maybe, as she was thirty-two years old, it was thought more likely that there would be problems with a first pregnancy at that age and it was a case of better safe than sorry.

As far as Jim knows the fears were groundless. The birth must have gone well. As with all first babies it was no doubt very painful for his mum, but he seems to have emerged undamaged. His mum returned home where her own mother, who lived with her daughter and was always known to Jim as 'Gran', was able to offer support and advice, having reared six children of her own.

Meanwhile his dad, a teacher in a local school, was busy; he was always busy. Besides his teaching job and growing all the family's green food he, during the Second World War, devoted many evenings and weekends preparing with his Home Guard comrades for the defence of the beautiful Dorset countryside should Herr Hitler change his mind about the wisdom of invading from across the English Channel.

However in 1941 the Germans, after the rescue of so many of our troops at 'Dunkirk' and then finding themselves unable to defeat our brave 'few' airmen (though, fortunately unknown to them, they came perilously close to doing so), turned their efforts towards invading Russia. From then on Herr Hitler seemed content to concentrate on destroying our British towns and cities from the air. Weymouth was not spared, suffering many raids and much loss of life.

The British and its allies returned the compliment in good measure. For the first time in warfare twice as many of the wartime deaths were ordinary citizens not military personnel.

Civilian deaths were caused by the bombing of residential areas, the sinking of cargo ships, the murder of millions of Jews and the killing of internees by deliberate cruelty, starvation or overwork. Finally atomic bombs destroyed the population of two large Japanese cities where a vast number of fatalities were caused by radiation, the blast itself, or later through radiation sickness.

The treatment of Prisoners of War also often completely ignored the Geneva Conventions. The Japanese were outrageously harsh whilst the Germans, as they invaded Russia in 1941, murdered en masse thousands of innocent Russian peasants. In the winter of 1945, with the Russians advancing, German troops forced around 30 000 prisoners (no one is sure of precisely how many) to walk up to 1000 miles westward. Named 'The March' or 'The Long March' or, equally correctly, 'The Death March', thousands of those who started out did not survive to meet the Americans invading from the other direction. Those who died were lost to the cold, starvation and exhaustion, or were shot by their captors.

◆ ◆ ◆

This would be a short book if a Nazi bomb or bullet had had Jim's name on it but happily Jim, his mum and dad, and his hymn singing Gran came safely through the war, though not without a few near misses.

One night several bombs fell on the neighbouring street, the ruined buildings later providing Jim and his mates with an exciting back-drop for cops and robbers games without the participants giving much thought to the agony and loss suffered by the houses' occupants when one night some German bomber crew had a few spare bombs to dispose of before returning home. Nor did Jim think about how the same bombs dropping a second or two earlier, or possibly later, could well have seen his home in the same state and Jim probably no more, unless the table-like Morrison shelter proved more substantial than it appeared to be.

Not that this was Hitler's only attempt to spare generations yet to come the agony of Jim teaching them the joys of solving simultaneous equations as, sometime in late 1941, Jim and his mum were fortunate that a German pilot was a bad shot when he raked with machine-gun bullets the road where his mum was pushing him in his pram.

Jim had been blissfully unaware of this, or of the danger he had been in during his early life, although his mum told him that as a baby he always cried bitterly when the waves of German bombers flew over.

His only personal memory of World War Two was when, in 1944, he recalls standing hand-in-hand with his mum while watching the seemingly endless parade of tanks roll down the main road towards their waiting ships in Portland Harbour as the invasion of Normandy progressed.

CHAPTER TWO

Ancestor Worship: Female Side

Perhaps while Jim is sleeping, and crying, through the first few years of his life it gives me a chance to tell you about his ancestors.

His mum's father was a head gardener in a local private residence. Her own mother was from a family of farm workers in Buckland Ripers, a small village between Weymouth and Abbotsbury.

Jim visited Buckland Riper's churchyard later in his life and found the tombstones of several of his ancestors, all of whom lived to a prodigious old age for their time. This is something that has continued down the ages so that if one of Jim's mum's family died without reaching ninety they were regarded as having 'died young'. So far none have made the century but Jim tells me that he intends to give it a good try!

Jim's mum had two brothers and three sisters but she was the only one to gain a grant to go to Weymouth Grammar School then, after passing the matriculation examination, qualifying to go on to higher education. There were not many white-collar jobs available to females in the early nineteen-hundreds; mainly the choice was nursing or teaching. She decided on teaching and so enrolled at Sainsbury Diocesan Training College.

She later told her son how the students were very closely chaperoned and that the only time they saw men was during their weekly Sunday service across the green at the cathedral where a girl could imagine having a passionate affair with a handsome young clergyman. Some chance of that!

After qualifying at Salisbury College Jim's mum gained a temporary teaching post in a village in Somerset where she fell for Jimmie, the son of her landlady. The romance, if romance it was, lasted only for a term before she moved to a permanent job in Bristol. However she carried a candle for her first love all her life, though the distance between them and no easy means of travel from the city to an isolated village meant that they never met again.

Many years later Jim took his mother, then in her eighties and widowed, to the village, but they found that her Jimmie had died some years before their visit. They left some flowers on his grave.

The time Jim's mum spent in her Bristol teaching employment was also short as she had not been long there when she received a telegram informing her that her father had died.

He was a head gardener and in the course of his work he had cut his knee. At first this did not seem serious but when his knee became swollen he went to the doctor who diagnosed 'housemaid's knee', thus failing to identify the cause which was that a bacterial infection had set in.

We are in the late nineteen-twenties and the marvel of penicillin's fatal effect on bacteria had only just been discovered by Alexander Fleming who had left a petri dish of bacteria lying open on his desk while he went on holiday, as one does, well as Alexander Fleming did anyway.

On his return he noticed that whilst he was enjoying the Scottish sunshine (if he was that lucky) the bacteria in the dish had also enjoyed their free time; in their case by reproducing themselves, although those close to a mould that had grown on the edge of the dish seemed to have lived dangerously and had been eliminated.

"Let's see if this mould has had an effect on my bacteria." is not the average person's reaction to finding a less than spotless kitchen on return from a vacation in Scotland, but Fleming's decision to investigate eventually saved millions of humans, not to mention animals, from a painful death.

He found the mould did, in fact, kill bacteria, wrote a paper about it which was published in the British Journal of Experimental Pathology (on everyone's must read list – not!) and chose to name his mould 'Penicillin'. Any such a mould is of the species named 'penicillium' as apparently it resembles a paint-brush which is penicillium in Greek. If you like Blue Stilton cheese, the mould in that is of the same family. I hope this has not put you off your supper.

Fleming continued to experiment with his penicillin but could only produce small quantities of it. He thought if it could be grown in sufficient quantity it would most likely be useful as an antiseptic or as an aid to bacterial research. Although he did try injecting it into healthy mice to see if it made them ill, which it didn't, it seems he did not then try infecting a mouse with bacteria to see if the penicillin would attack the bacteria when it was in their bodies.

Rather an oversight.

However some time later his discovery came to the notice of a team at Oxford University led by Howard Florey, Ernst Chain and Norman Heatley. They worked out how to produce and refine enough penicillin for it to be of some medical use.

It was not until September 1940 in Salisbury that it was first tried out, on an infection caused by bacteria getting into a policeman's body through a minor cut while he was gardening, just like Jim's grandfather. The penicillin was immediately effective but there was not enough of it to continue the treatment. When the team ran out of it the man became ill again and died.

With the need to fight a war taking precedence over everything else, Florey and Heatley decided that their best chance of being able to produce penicillin in large quantities lay in the USA who at that time, before the Japanese attack on their ships in Pearl Harbour, were neutral. So in 1941 they flew there to continue their efforts with the support of a large drug company.

There in 1942 an alternative source of the antibiotic was found on a mouldy cantaloupe melon bought in the local market by a lab assistant. She had been on the lookout for growths on rotten fruit and this source proved to yield far more penicillin than Fleming's original mould.

The researchers made good progress in producing large quantities of it so that by the end of the war it was saving many lives on and off the battlefield.

Unfortunately for Jim's grandad he was living in pre-antibiotic days and, once cellulitis took hold, there was no cure and he died within a few days.

Jim was to revisit the effects of cellulitis himself later in his life but is alive to tell the tale. He thanks you Alexander.

I guess Jim has another reason to be grateful to Dr Fleming's failure to make the most of his discovery as, following the death of her father, his mum was summoned back home where she was needed to help run the house and their smallholding. She was soon appointed as a teacher at the local elementary school where she was joined a few years later by Jim's dad when he was appointed to the same establishment.

In view of Jim's conception it seems that Jim's dad must have liked the look of Florrie and probably vice versa. However a romance was certainly not expected, or indeed permitted, between school teacher colleagues in those days. Jim was only much later told the dramatic story of how his parents came to marry, facing much trauma and having to overcome many obstacles along the way. I will tell all when Jim reaches the age at which his parents were cornered into having to tell their children their somewhat tragic but eventually 'happy ever after' story.

CHAPTER THREE

Ancestor Worship: Male Side

Jim's dad, Dene, was born in Portsmouth in 1905.

In spite of what you have just read, Jim's dad's name was not Dene.

In fact it was Harold Christopher but apparently an aunt refused to call him Harold and substituted Dene, for reasons lost in the mists of time. Jim's mum never called him Harold and Jim thought that his dad was not fond of his baptismal name and preferred to be a Dene.

He was of that fortunate group who were too young to fight in the 1914-18 war and, unless the country was in extreme need, too old to be called up in the 1939-46 one.

The earliest Jim knows of his ancestors on his father's side is of his Great-Great-Grandfather, Roger, and his wife.

Roger was born in Cornwall and became a coastguard. After finishing his training he was appointed to guard the coast of Cork in Ireland. Then of course, though not through the native Irish's choice, all of Ireland was part of Great Britain.

In Cork he met, and fell madly in love with, a daughter of a prosperous Irish land-owner. The love-birds wanted to marry but the girl's family had better prospects for her than marrying a lowly coastguard, not to mention an English one, and they would not give their consent to the marriage.

However Roger's passion for his girl must have been reciprocated and the pair refused to give each other up. One day, or possibly one night, they eloped back to Hayle in Cornwall where they married.

How romantic was that!

The 'heiress', as her descendant's always called her, was cut out of her father's will but was not entirely cut off from her Irish family and she received a quarterly allowance until her death.

They had three children, all boys. One, Valentine, became a sailor but drowned when his ship went down in heavy seas off the coast. Jim knows nothing of the middle son, John, but the youngest was Jim's great-grandad, Henry. His trade was a ship-wright. As was usual at this time the ships he worked on would have been of wood and probably fairly small ones suitable for coastal use.

Henry met and married Jane Christopher Rouse, a girl from St Ives.

When a young girl in 1848 she stitched a large tapestry. This heirloom is much treasured by Jim and his family. It shows an exotic bird in flight through a cloud of flowers. and bears her name as Jane C. Rouse. Why a girl was given the name Christopher is a mystery and what Jane made of having a male second name we shall never know. As the tapestry does not have the space to show the full name in the size letters she chose to use it is hard to know whether reducing her middle name to just C. was deliberate or forced on her by the design of the tapestry.

Soon after their marriage Henry lost his job when the ship-builder went bankrupt. Perhaps the development of iron ships made wooden ones less popular or maybe his bosses got their sums wrong.

He could not find new employment in Cornwall and, as he later told Jim's dad, he decided to go to Portsmouth to see if he could find employment in ship-building there.

Being out of work he was unable to afford to pay for this journey and so he walked to Portsmouth.

Apparently there was a toll gate at Bursledon, not many miles from Portsmouth. Henry was unable to pay the toll and when telling his story many years later to Jim's dad he admitted that he had vaulted the gate in the dark and so come safely to his destination.

As I have done several times in putting this tale together I thought that this needed checking out and the internet, where else, had a description of the gate and a photo to prove it, though it looks rather high to be climbed over!

Whether by sneaking though or climbing over, Henry made it to Portsmouth and obtained work in the dockyard there. Jane Christopher joined him, though I guess she took the train. I assume that Henry would have earnt enough to send the money for the fare or maybe her parents paid for a ticket. Not to mention the long walk, Victorian skirts would have made vaulting the Bursledon gate even more of a challenge for Jane than it must have been for her husband.

Once together again Henry and Jane rented rooms and in due course had two sons. One of them, James Henry, was to be Jim's grandfather, always known to Jim as 'Pa'. The other son, William, joined the merchant navy.

Finding his dockyard pay needed topping up Henry took out a mortgage on a house in Lake Road and converted the front room into a dairy shop. Jane, with Pa's help after he had left school, ran the shop thus launching the business side of Jim's family. Besides the shop sales they also delivered fresh dairy produce to the dockyard and to houses in the area.

Tragedy lay ahead though as while Pa was in his early twenties Jane, his mother, fell and broke her hip. With modern treatments not available she did not recover from this and died shortly after.

Pa, Jim's grandad, felt the loss of his mum very deeply and even as an old man could not talk about her without breaking down in tears.

Henry re-married and he, with his second wife, ran the grocery shop until, after both their deaths, it was left to Pa who let it out. In time it was converted to a small restaurant, the Cinderella Café, which Jim and his sister inherited on Pa's death.

Retracing our steps a little, Pa helped with his father's dairy shop for a few years after he left school but then decided to buy a tobacconist's business in Kingston Road.

Whilst running this he met and married Emma Matilda, Jim's paternal grandmother, known to Jim as Nannie.

Emma had been told by a cousin that she was a descendant of Oliver Cromwell's famous 17th Century Admiral Blake, the Somerset born 'Father of the Royal Navy'. The cousin's middle name was indeed Blake and she possessed a pointed 'bicorn' hat which was claimed to have belonged to the admiral.

Looking through many portraits of the said admiral I cannot find any in which he is wearing a hat of any description so it is hard to know if that could be true. Then, maybe he was hatless when sitting for his painter because he had given his hat to one of Jim's ancestors!

Be that as it may, what is certain is that James Henry ('Pa') and Emma ('Nannie') set up home in Essex Road.

Later Pa added to his tobacconist business with a confectioner's further along Kingston Road and so started learning how to make home-made sweets.

Pa was a shrewd businessman and one day he noticed a baker's shop on Fratton Bridge which was looking the worse for wear. He spoke to the owner and offered to buy the business from him. This was agreed and the shop changed to a second sweet shop and this did well with Pa and Nannie in charge.

Thanks partly to Sunlight soap (|I'll explain later), Pa was eventually able to buy his rented properties and when he retired he still enjoyed the income from his let shops. He also had enough savings to buy an acre or so of land on which he built a bungalow, developing the remaining part into an apple orchard and a smallholding, complete with chickens and tobacco plants.

The tobacco plants were not a great success in the English climate but Jim never forgot the toxic smell of the leaves drying on the ceiling beams in his Pa's wooden outbuilding. Jim has no knowledge of whether they ever came to fill a clay pipe. He rather hopes not.

In retirement Pa continued to exhibit his profit-making skills as he sold his produce, though not we guess his tobacco, from a stall on the main road which passed his property. One trick which he used to tempt folk to buy his wares was to invent new names for old varieties of apples so that folk could try the latest 'improved' (or not) variety.

One family trait that Pa suffered from has passed through to Jim; both had hearing loss as old age came in. Modern hearing aids are a huge help but in Pa's day they were large and not very good. Pa refused to use his, preferring Jim's alternative solution of a rolled up sheet of card to make an ear trumpet which he held against his wireless speaker to listen to the news.

Jim comments, "Don't you often wish you could speak at length to the dead and get them to fill in all the details of a life now just marked by a few isolated happenings and official documents but with no idea of the how and why? Well perhaps not so true of one's life if you are royalty but my family certainly isn't that, although I did once come within touching distance of Prince Charles at a Buckingham Palace Garden Party."

Thank you Jim for butting in but maybe, as you are allowing me to tell your life story, you are going some way to fill in some of those blanks for those of your family yet to come.

CHAPTER FOUR

False Teeth

Now where was I? Oh yes, I need to explain how it was that Jim's father, Dene, was a school-teacher in Weymouth when Jim was born, rather than running his father's chain of shops in Portsmouth.

Indeed Dene was expected in due course to take over the business and he had to leave school to help his father as soon as he reached the minimum leaving age of fourteen years. He therefore had no qualifications on paper but became skilled in the art of sweet-making whilst his mum and dad ran the shops, opening early to catch folk on their way to work and staying open late to catch the pub trade after the drinkers were turned out.

Making a profit was always uppermost in Pa's mind.

Jim's dad told him, when he later recorded memories of his life, that he was instructed to ignore the sweet-makers' guide book's recipe for nut chocolate by increasing the nuts to chocolate ratio in the bars he made. This much pleased the customers who commented how wonderfully nutty their purchased chocolate bars were but were perhaps not aware that nuts were much cheaper per pound than was chocolate.

Whilst I was writing the above my granddaughter arrived and presented me with a bar of Lindt nut chocolate (see back cover) which proudly proclaims that it contains 34% hazel nuts.

The spirit of Jim's grandfather lives on!

Great empires can be built on simple ideas and Pa struck gold by taking advantage of a sales promotion by the Sunlight soap company, Lever Brothers.

They would send you a free bar of soap, or a box of soap powder, when you sent them a certain (quite large) number of their wrappers. It took ages for one person to collect enough wrappers and then they had to go to the trouble of sending them off.

Realising that this was a hassle for many people, Jim's grandad offered the whole population of Portsmouth and neighbouring towns a small sum, usually paid in postage stamps, for each single wrapper brought to his shops. He then negotiated with Sunlight to supply the soap to him when he had collected a large number of wrappers.

Initially the soap received was sold on in the shops but his enterprise was so successful that their house became overloaded with boxes from Sunlight. To overcome this Pa negotiated a deal whereby the soap was sent direct to a wholesaler who then paid Pa.

The income from this venture enabled Pa to purchase the buildings which he had previously only rented and so he ended up owning three business properties and his own house, all of which he let to provide his pension when he eventually retired himself in the mid 1930's.

Another likely tale I thought, like Admiral Blake's hat,

and typed 'Sunlight Soap Wrapper' into Google.

Up came an 1895 label sold in 2020 on E-bay for £11. This label offered the purchaser (in 1895) a book in return for a number of wrappers sent to them and suggests clergymen collect wrappers in bulk from their congregation and so build a lending library.

It seems highly likely that in due course the offer changed to the 'gift' being another bar of soap or box of soap powder rather than a book, or maybe Pa negotiated this himself.

I thought that I would check this out with Lever Brothers, now merged into Unilever, and they kindly had a look through their archives but they could not find any reference to Jim's grandad.

They did say that personal records were destroyed once they were no longer relevant so I guess we just accept that the story is true.

However the long hours and the sweaty labour over caldrons of boiling sugar behind the shop was not to Jim's dad's liking. Nor was his father's insistence on early morning openings and late night closings.

One day Pa broke his false teeth (possibly sampling too many bars of nut toffee) and visited a dentist.

Chatting to the dentist while he waited for the repair to be carried out he told him that his son was not happy with his life and the dentist suggested that he should enrol in the local higher education college, gain the necessary qualifications, and then train as a dentist himself.

When Pa came home he told Jim's dad of this suggestion and they agreed that he would do just that.

Although no doubt a disappointment to Pa, it is very much to his credit that he put his son's happiness above the future of his business, though he may have been well aware that his son's business acumen was not his strongest suit.

Unfortunately this well intentioned plan led to a lot of heartache over the years to come as you will find out in due course.

Jim's dad may not have had the ability, or maybe just not the desire, to run a business but he had a high intelligence and a capacity for hard work. No surprise then that at the end of his course he gained the necessary qualifications to go on to further education.

The prospect of spending all day inside the mouths of strangers seemed less than appealing to him.

He decided instead to train as a teacher.

He was talented with his hands so at college studied woodwork, making all the furniture that Jim would later grow up with. I do mean all. Every piece of furniture in Jim's house had been made by his dad, who also built a treadle lathe so that he could turn spindles, egg cups, bowls etc.

This furniture, much of it in oak, lives on.

After two year's teacher training Jim's dad qualified and was appointed a woodwork teacher at an Elementary (up to 14+) school in the outskirts of Weymouth where he remained for many years.

Jim never discovered quite when his dad's musical skills developed but his philosophy was ever that if another man can do something then so could he, so somehow he became a skilled amateur violinist and cellist.

His headmaster, Mr Dominey, was himself a keen musician. He started a school orchestra with Jim's dad as the Leader. They won awards at Bournemouth Music Festivals and became close friends.

The orchestra sadly came to an end when the 1944 Education Act changed the system and the school became a Junior School for 7 to 11 years old.

Further, as woodwork was no longer to be taught until the secondary stage, Jim's dad would either have to change schools or become a general subjects' teacher. He decided to take the second option and took on the top class of 10 and 11 year olds.

A few years later Jim found himself in his dad's class and was evermore full of admiration for his father's talent at passing on his knowledge to him and his classmates.

CHAPTER FIVE

And So To School

Whilst you have been reading of the life and times of Jim's ancestors our own time has moved on and Jim has come safely through the war years. He has acquired a much adored baby sister and narrowly avoided becoming a member of a one-parent family due to the impetuousness of their milkman.

Jim's dad, as you may recall, was in his mid-thirties when war broke out in 1939. With his age counting against him, as well as being in the teaching profession, he was not called to active service in the struggle to defeat Herr Hitler.

He nevertheless wanted to do his bit to save England from the Nazis so he joined the Home Guard.

Among the many activities to be practised in the group's preparations for imminent invasion was how to accost and capture any Germans foolhardy enough to parachute into territory protected by the Weymouth Home Guard Division.

To avoid slaughtering friend rather than foe there was a password system.

This led to Jim's dad experiencing an incident that could well have been straight out of a 'Dad's Army' episode.

The scene is the parish-church graveyard. The time is just after midnight. The Home Guard is on guard, as you might expect them to be.

In the pitch black of the war years enter Jim's father doing the rounds to check up on the rest of the troop.

He thought the most danger he would be in was to trip over

a grave, fall into an open one, or walk into an invisible grave-stone.

He had avoided all these perils, only to be hit in the chest at point blank range by a round fired by a fellow volunteer, his milkman, whose policy seems to have been 'Shoot first, ask for the password after.'

Fortunately for Jim's dad the milkman's rifle was loaded with blanks so, although he was badly bruised, the injury was not life-threatening. What Jim's dad said to the milkman is not recorded, which is probably just as well or I may have needed to insert some blanks of my own if he had, as would be entirely forgivable, perhaps let rip with "You b*****!".

Suffice to say that the milkman was dismissed from the troop while Jim's dad changed his milk supplier and never again spoke to his home guard ex-colleague.

In case you are wondering, according to the internet, although blanks are less dangerous than live ammunition (fancy that!) they are far from harmless. Besides the hot combustion gases, any objects in the cartridge itself (like wadding or a bullet-shaped plug keeping the propellant in place) or indeed any object placed in the barrel, will be propelled at high velocity and will cause injury if fired at close range.

Another feature of 'Dad's Army' was also shared by Jim's family as one of his dad's ex-pupils was a Home Guard volunteer. Jim does not know why he was not called up; perhaps like Pike he had a 'weak chest'. He worked for the local butcher and on many a Saturday would appear at Jim's father's house door bearing a gift of sausages or offal, wrapped in white paper. Jim always knew him as 'The Sausage Boy' rather than 'Corporal Jones'.

He kept in touch with Jim's dad for many years after the war, though the eventual end of rationing saw the end of his 'under the counter' activity.

As he grew older Jim began to exhibit signs of being something of a show-off. Jim's mum later told him he was known to sing nursery rhymes to entertain, or more likely annoy, bus passengers when on a shopping trip with her.

He claims that he has no memory of doing any such thing but, as I said, his mum was never caught out telling a lie (there really being a Father Christmas excepted; Jim was most upset when he was told by some older girls that Santa was a fantasy character).

Considering the evidence, being writ large in the story of his life over many years, of Jim's propensity for entertaining any audience he can gather in front of him, whether by an unfortunate accident of chance or by choice and possibly, hopefully, including you reading this book, I think we must accept that Jim is guilty as charged.

The war came to an end and at just over five years old Jim was due to start at infant school, which was in the same building as the one in which his dad taught.

Jim however did not think much of his freedom being curtailed by having to be in a classroom with forty other children and then having to do as he was told. When his dad deposited him with a rather forbidding female teacher and left to teach in his own classroom young Jim took the first opportunity to escape and ran home to his mother.

Jim cannot remember when or how he was returned to the school but it will not surprise you to learn that he was.

He soon settled down to being a schoolboy. With a teacher for a mother he was ahead of many of his classmates in the three r's (reading, 'riting and 'rthmetic; not that calling this the three 'r's would encourage pupils to spell correctly).

This pre-school home tuition got him into trouble.

Once a week Jim's class was supervised by Miss Dyke. Each pupil was given a copy of the same book and in turn had to read a passage aloud whilst the other pupils followed it in silence.

Woe betide any pupil found to be reading ahead of where the orator was.

One day a pupil was struggling with a difficult word and Jim's patience snapped; he offered assistance by pronouncing the word for him.

This incurred great wrath from Miss Dyke who proceeded to give Jim a verbal lashing.

He was fortunate that it was just a verbal one, for many of the teachers in those days were all too pleased to indulge in some sadistic physical punishment.

Jim protested that he was only trying to help his classmate, for which justification his 'fifty lines' increased to a hundred, causing Jim to exclaim "Oh bother you Miss Dyke!" and so got them doubled again.

Never one to take things lying down Jim added fuel to the fire by going up to the teacher at the end of the lesson and asking if it was OK if he wrote his lines on a typewriter!

I am sure you can imagine the response he got to that but he learned his lesson the hard way, as he did all his life, and never sinned, at least not in that way, ever again.

However Jim's love of the typewriter got him into another bother, this time centred on fish. In fact fish seemed to cause him several embarrassing incidents over the years.

This one was a result of a class visit to see an aquarium at another school. This had been arranged by Jim's infant school headmistress. She selected Jim to be the pupil who would write the thank-you letter to the other school, which he did.

However when the headmistress came to read what he had written she was horrified to find that Jim had committed a dreadful sin.

Instead of the prescribed way of writing a letter 'a', that is with one upright and one half circle, Jim had adopted the typewritten variety, such as you have been reading and will continue to read throughout this book.

'Yah Boo to you Mrs Briggs.' thought Jim when in old age he reflected that not just typewriters but computers, i-phones and just about every piece of print in existence uses the design of 'a' that he was, as a six-year old, in deep trouble for daring to use in a handwritten letter.

Jim was ordered to write his thank-you letter again but, try as he might, he still managed to get at least one typewriter version of an 'a' into his submission. It took many goes and more than a few tears before a 'faultless' copy was produced.

Jim's handwriting was a problem ever after.

When he was eleven he was punished during a Christmas holiday by a concerned teacher. His punishment for his untidy calligraphy was to write out the whole of Charles Dickens' book 'A Christmas Carol' in his 'best' handwriting.

Needless to say this did little to improve it.

Maybe though it inspired his later role as a successful author, although he had already started keeping a record of his experiences and his innermost thoughts as soon as learnt to write.

In a home-made diary which he treasured all his life he wrote, 'I have a sister. I do love my baby sister.' and so he did, and never stopped loving her for the rest of his life.

However he is sorry to report that the 'a's' he wrote in the above two sentences would not best please Mrs Briggs!

CHAPTER SIX

The Mad Hatter Falls For Alice

It was at about this time that Jim had yet another incident in his large catalogue of dodgy moments, though for once through no fault of his own, unless being a gullible fool counts as a fault.

During the war the council had dug at the side of the main road a large open cistern, lined with concrete, which was kept filled with water in case an incendiary bomb set any local houses ablaze. By the time Jim was old enough to be out on his own, and with the war won, the cistern was no longer a swimming-pool. Instead it was just an attraction for fly-tipping, along with puddles of rainwater which I am sure were much appreciated by the local mosquitoes.

One day some local lads persuaded Jim to stand on the rim to look into the cistern. He cannot remember what the lure was but whatever it was Jim fell for it in more ways than one as the next thing he knew he had been pushed over the edge.

The culprits left the scene laughing merrily at their trick whilst Jim found himself a trifle wet but fortunately unharmed. However he was completely unable to get out of the cistern which was far deeper than he was tall. After a while his cries for help were heard by a passing pedestrian who got hold of a ladder and so rescued him and took him home to his mother.

No harm done and another lesson learned the hard way.

Generally though Jim enjoyed his infant school days. He loved reading and amongst the classroom library was 'The Story of Little Black Sambo'. This is very much not 'Black Lives Matter' approved. There was only one 'black' living near him and he, shockingly (I hope) to you in the twenty-first century, was always known as 'Darky Carter'.

Maybe this was no worse than when many years later Jim taught for a year in a predominantly black area in the Caribbean where the youngsters would call out 'Whitey' as he passed them. Whatever, there were certainly no other black faces to be seen, either among his school mates or indeed during his whole life until he went to live in the Midlands in his early twenties.

Amongst Jim's classmates was one who he adored. She was called Irene and was the daughter of the school secretary. Her father had been killed in the war. Jim's dad was a good friend to her mother. In fact Jim thinks that maybe his mother thought his dad was too good a friend!

Whatever, Jim and Irene always went to each other's parties and Jim 'fancied the pants off her' as the saying goes. It remained just a saying but you can imagine Jim's joy was unbounded when his class put on a play version of the Tea Party from 'Alice in Wonderland' and Irene took on the role of Alice whilst Jim, type-cast of course, took the role of The Mad Hatter', complete with the ten-and-sixpence label on his hat.

Jim's life might have turned out very differently if Irene had continued to be a schoolmate at his mixed-sex Grammar School once his hormones fully kicked in, but her mother, maybe wisely, sent her to a girls-only school in another town. Although a few years later their paths crossed once more Jim was by then deeply in love with Julia, the girl who was to become his wife and the mother of his children.

Life's way is littered with 'what-ifs'; the road ahead branching left or right and, sometimes by one's own choice, sometimes by that of others, one's destiny is thus fixed with no option to turn about and try the other way.

Jim's lifelong experience would be no different.

Enough of philosophy! Jim has reached the grand age of seven and has moved into the Junior School where he would be for the next four years. These years were mainly pleasant enough and they passed fairly incident free. He learnt to play the piano and joined a church choir. However this last role was the cause of not such a pleasant experience.

The older choir boys put the new younger ones through an induction ceremony which involved being thrown down a grassy slope towards the back of the church. This was no doubt not likely to do much harm but Jim was frightened of the experience and took to his heels, running home to his mum and dad in a blue funk. His dad, ever the teacher, set off the next morning to give the head choirboy a severe dressing down for so upsetting his son.

Whether this was the best way to deal with his cowardly offspring is something for you to consider but, although it hardly made Jim a popular member of the choir, he was thereafter spared the induction experience so has no way of knowing whether it was as dreadful an ordeal as he feared it would be.

As you know, Jim's dad was a talented violinist and was the leader of a string quartet which met in the evenings at his home. Many was the night Jim went to sleep, wrapped up under the eiderdown in his cold bedroom, lullabied by the sound of one of Mozart's or Beethoven's chamber-music works.

By golly though, were the winter bedrooms cold in those days. The house only had a fire-place in the two downstairs rooms and before going to bed a stone-ware hot-water bottle wrapped in its own hand-knitted jacket was placed in the bed. This somewhat took the edge off the shock of climbing in.

Frost on the inside of the window panes was common throughout those 1940's winters.

The school played football matches with other schools in the area some weekends and for some inexplicable reason Jim was appointed as chief reporter on each match, delivering his report at the Monday assembly.

Jim is certain his reports were sadly lacking in quality as he had, and has, no interest in the sport.

He had no way of knowing how well each team was playing. In fact the only thing he was fairly sure about was which side scored the most goals.

As for the off-side rule, this was, and has remained, a mystery to him although he did much later in his life find in his change a comparatively rare 50p coin issued as part of the 2016 Great Britain Olympic Games which seemed to be attempting to explain it. It failed in its intent as far as Jim is concerned but he was pleased to find that it was much sought after and he sold it on E-bay to a delighted collector for a price far in excess of its stated value.

These were the days when 'The Eleven Plus' loomed large in the minds of many British pupils and their teachers at the end of Junior School. It was a major fork in the road to adulthood. Do we go Left or Right? Not the child's decision though; one's future was decided by how well one had learnt to do repetitive arithmetic and be able to pick the right answer in so called 'Intelligence' tests. Thus at ten or eleven years of age a pupil's future role in life was settled: Grammar School (destined for the professions) or the dreaded 'Secondary Modern' (destined for manual labour).

There was a loop-hole two years later whereby, if it became clear to one's teachers that one had somehow ended up in the wrong type of education, pupils could change schools. However it was very few pupils who actually made the switch. On one side parents were understandably loathe to have their darlings move from a Grammar School to a Secondary Modern or even a 'Technical College'. They could raise an objection to the suggested move and if persistent they were often listened to. On the other side this meant that those pupils who their teachers thought should move the other way were stymied by the lack of available places in the Grammar School.

Comprehensive education is not perfect but it is so much fairer to all than the system Jim lived through in his schooldays.

Jim's Junior School was different to most as the headmaster would not indulge in the 'practising to pass the eleven-plus' that so many other schools adopted. Apart from one 'mock' test session, Jim's rounded education was not influenced by 'teaching to the test'. This meant that the percentage of pupils at his school who 'passed' was much lower than in schools where lots of practice papers were worked. Although admirable in giving Jim the much wider and more enjoyable education that he had in his dad's class this was not so popular with the school governors and it was changed to 'teaching to pass the test' when a new headmaster was appointed a few years later.

Does this not make you think of the tragic effect on a wider, broader education when the Tory's government instigated the testing regime that was part of 'The National Curriculum' introduced in the 1990's?

Don't answer that!

CHAPTER SEVEN

Jim's Long Lost Sister

Jim was in his last year at Junior School when the sad news came on the radio that King George the Sixth, still only in his late fifties but known to be somewhat unwell, had died suddenly in his sleep.

For the adults who had been through the war, with their king and queen boosting morale by refusing to leave their home in Buckingham Palace in spite of several bombs being dropped on it, the king was held in great affection. The whole country was shocked and went into deep mourning.

The school closed for the following day and Jim had an unexpected holiday.

Being blissfully ignorant of how fortunate he was not to be in the Hitlerjugend (Nazi Youth), our Jim was not as saddened at the news as his parents were and thought that he should be as well. Instead he was happy to have a day off school and was given a good telling off for not being in mourning at the death of his king.

He remembers subsequently going to sit on the back steps of his home, cuddling his pet rabbit ('Silkypaws') and crying, although more with shame at not being sufficiently upset than by the sad news of the death of his country's beloved monarch.

As I write the news has come on the radio of the death of the Prince Philip, Duke of Edinburgh and, though hardly a huge shock when he was close to a hundred years old, I can understand how upset Jim's parents were. He and our queen have been there all my adult life.

◆ ◆ ◆

Jim's last year at Junior School was memorable, but not always in a good way, as it was then that he was told about the circumstances that led up to his parents' marriage.

Jim's mum was suffering with a 'bad back'. The treatment for this in those days was complete bed-rest so a bed was brought downstairs for her to lie there, probably for weeks, to await recovery. Jim's dad and his Gran took over the household chores, though by then Gran was beginning to start the descent into dementia of which more later when Jim found himself in further trouble.

Although his mum's back was undoubtedly very painful it was not this that caused so much heartache; it was that Rosemary had written to her dad and wanted to meet him.

You may think that you have not been paying sufficient attention as you do not know who Rosemary is.

No, it is not just you that have been kept in ignorance. It came as a complete surprise to Jim as well. Besides having a (much loved) sister he also had a half-sister, for that is who Rosemary turned out to be.

On this memorable day, his mum in bed and in tears, his dad almost in despair, Jim was only given the briefest of facts. It was only after his father died that he gradually pieced the story together with the help of his mother and the recollections of a cousin who had known both Rosemary and her mother.

As you may remember, Jim's dad, fed up with the long hours and sweated labour of the sweets and tobacco (and soap!) shop, went back to a mixed college in his twenties.

There is a thread of 'devil may care' passion running through Jim's family history. After all, his great-great-grandfather, Roger, had eloped rather than give up the love of his life. Jim's dad must have been just as susceptible to the attractions of the opposite sex, falling head over heels in love with Phyllis, a young girl at the college.

A fog descends over how their relationship developed as from that day onward his dad never mentioned the subject again. What is certain is that they married before he went to teachers' training college and Phyllis lodged with her father-in-law and mother-in-law at their smallholding. Whenever he could get away from college Jim's dad used to cycle the twenty miles each way to spend time with his young wife.

On completing his training he was appointed to a teaching post in Weymouth. He found lodgings near the school and he and Phyllis moved to live in Dorset.

School years then, as now, started in September and it was getting towards their first Christmas in Dorset when Jim's dad came home from school one day to be greeted at the door by his shocked landlady with the news that his pregnant wife had packed her bags and had gone. Jim's mum later told him that apparently a clergyman gave her a home, for a while at least. Jim felt his mum wondered if there was more than pure Christian kindness in the clergyman's involvement with Phyllis.

Be that as it may, in due course her daughter, Rosemary, was born. Jim's dad paid his estranged wife an allowance to help cover the expense of rearing a child as a single mother. This explains why Jim's parents never had any spare money until Rosemary reached her twenty-first birthday.

That December morning all those years' ago was, as far as Jim knows, the last his dad saw of Phyllis, his wife, and until this fateful day he had, again as far as Jim knows, never seen his daughter, although in those pre-DNA testing days he was not absolutely certain that she was indeed his offspring. However Jim was later sent a photo of Rosemary in her early twenties and he could see a striking family resemblance so he does not think the matter is in any doubt.

CHAPTER EIGHT

"Oh, Mr Wright!"

The years passed by until, in 1937, new divorce laws came into effect. It was no longer necessary to prove adultery. Instead divorce could be granted for 'cruelty, desertion, or incurable insanity'. Agreeing on the definitions of 'cruelty' and especially 'incurable insanity' must have kept many lawyers expensively occupied for years, but desertion seems simpler to define.

Jim's grandad, Pa, discussed this with his son and persuaded him that he had indeed been 'deserted' and could therefore file for divorce.

This was enacted and Jim's dad found himself once again a bachelor. It must have been a very difficult time for him and his parents but as the subject was not ever discussed you will have to imagine the pain and suffering for yourself.

Once the divorce papers arrived we could hope that the way forward would now be sweetness and light. Maybe it would be in these more enlightened times when you are reading this but then, in 1937, although a no blame or at least a 'no adultery needing to be proved' divorce was at last permitted, it was still a reason for great shame and embarrassment. More, much more, sorrow lay ahead.

In his late thirties Jim's newly single dad acquired a car and he made the occasional journey to Southampton to visit his parents and his sister. On learning that Jim's mum, Florrie, who you will remember taught in the same school, had a sister in Portsmouth he offered to take his colleague to visit her as he was going that way the next weekend.

This seemed to Florrie to be a good idea so they set off. Crossing the New Forest, Jim's dad told Florrie the story of how William the Conqueror's son, Rufus (also he of Rufus Castle if you know Church Ope on the Isle of Portland) was killed by an (accidental?) arrow shot ostensibly at a deer. A memorial stone had been erected to mark the spot (search Google to learn more of this fascinating story).

Would Florrie like to see the aforesaid monument?

She would!

So they set off down the track to the very spot, whereupon Jim's dad, impetuously and utterly unexpectedly, got down on one knee and asked Florrie to marry him.

Jim's mum's response went down in family history, brief though it was.

"Oh, Mr Wright!"

She was utterly shocked by this proposal from a man she had only previously thought of as a fellow teacher, not even as a close friend, and certainly not as a husband.

One can only imagine the thoughts going through Florrie's mind on the rest of that journey let alone the conversation she must have had with her sister at whose home she stayed for the weekend.

On the Sunday Jim's dad picked her up for the car ride back to Weymouth. What they said to each other on this return journey, which took several hours, Jim does not know and we leave to your imagination although Florrie was capable of long periods of tight-lipped silence so maybe they both said very little.

As a single female in her early thirties she was not averse to the prospect of marriage and starting a family but to consider marriage in those days to a man she hardly knew, let alone a divorced man she hardly knew, must have been another matter.

Jim's dad was never one to give up once he started on something. Not a bad fault, if fault it is, but sometimes one is one's own worst enemy; when trapped in a hole don't keep digging.

Jim would tell the story of how, when his own first car needed, and had indeed been already fitted with, a replacement brake cylinder due to the original one having seized up solid, his dad insisted on getting the faulty one to come to bits. This involved much use of a blow-torch and a large hammer and took some considerable time. To what purpose was not entirely clear to Jim but I guess it made some sort of sense to his dad.

So, as I was saying, Jim's dad did not give up. He persevered with his determination to win Florrie over. He continued to press his suit on her, coming perilously close to giving her a full-blown nervous breakdown.

However she must have been won round eventually. Then all hell broke loose.

She had to leave the school as marriage between two teachers, let alone one being a divorcee, was out of the question. In fact even employing any married woman was not permitted in many education authorities, including Dorset.

Then in came the full wrath of the Church of England. As with King Edward the Eighth, the Church would not countenance remarriage after divorce, nor permit divorced members of the congregation to take Holy Communion, which is known as an 'excommunication'. The local priest took this rule very seriously. Jim's devout mother was faced with having to decide between marriage or taking Holy Communion.

You already know what she decided as else Jim would not have been around to feature in this story but it must have been a terrible time for her.

Incidentally, although the Church of England has gradually

come to accept divorced and re-married divorcees, not all Church of England priests will officiate at a full marriage service, just 'blessing' a registry office one, the first marriage being 'before God for life'. Thankfully taking the sacraments is no longer a problem.

Determined to at least involve God in their marriage ceremony, Florrie's aunt, a Baptist, spoke to her pastor about the problem and he agreed to marry them in the Baptist Church. So they were duly wed, and a year or two later along came Jim.

All this came to light because of the request from Rosemary, the daughter of Jim's dad's brief first marriage, to meet him for the first time in her life.

It seems that Pa and his wife, Nannie, had celebrated their Golden Wedding anniversary which was reported in the local paper. Rosemary saw the report and realised it was her dad's parents that were being written about. The article mentioned that Nannie and Pa's son was now a teacher in Dorset, so she contacted the Education Department there and managed to find out Jim's dad's address.

Jim never found out what had happened to Rosemary's mum, Phyllis, or whether she and her daughter, or indeed she and her own mother, were close or estranged.

It was arranged to meet Rosemary in the New Forest; oh no, not again!

What was it about the New Forest and Jim's dad?

Anyway the meeting took place, so Jim briefly came to see his half-sister, though he has no memory of ever meeting her again. Rosemary sent Jim a small framed painting of a sunflower and the photo I mentioned before, but with his dad not prepared to discuss the subject that was it. However Jim's mum kept a diary which indicated that after Rosemary had made contact she had kept in touch with Jim's dad and they met, unknown to Jim, at least once more as in one diary entry his mum wrote that 'Dene rushed off to Southampton as there was a problem with Rose-mary.'

Jim's cousin Mavis gave him the rest of the story as she knew it. You may recall that Mavis would have met Rosemary's mother, Phyllis, when she was living with her grandparent's. Learning that Rosemary had made contact Mavis quickly got in touch with her and they met. They must have warmed to each other as with both of them being in their twenties they arranged to share a flat in Southampton.

The rest of the story is shrouded by the darkness Jim's dad formed around his past life but it is known that Rosemary had an illegitimate son. Tragically he was badly disabled and died, to be joined shortly after in the communion of those gone before by Rosemary herself when she committed suicide.

It remains a great sadness to Jim that, by the time his father died leaving the way open to try to get to know and perhaps support his half-sister, it was too late.

Don't stop reading. That is about the worst I have to tell in this story of Jim's life and there is sunshine and laughter ahead. This is not 'Froggy's Little Brother', which was a Victorian melo-dramatic book of misery, hardship and untimely tragic deaths, somehow owned by Jim's Gran and which, when mentioned be-tween Jim and his sister, perhaps as a comment on some de-pressing TV serial, told all with nothing more needing to be said!

The author wrote the book with the admirable aim of making its Victorian readers aware of the need to address the dreadful poverty not far from their comfortable homes. It is not only Jim and his sister that remember the sad tale as it is still available and features in the novel 'The Pursuit of Love' by Nancy Mit-ford when it is sold in a book shop. This came to light when the BBC serialized Nancy's book and it led to a least one letter about Froggy in the Radio Times.

CHAPTER NINE

Sex Education

Let's return to our own melodrama.

As more understanding and tolerant times came in and with a new vicar appointed, the church opened its doors again to Jim's mum and dad and they both lived long and, Jim thinks, generally happy lives.

When tensions came, as they must in every marriage, Jim's mum advised him that the best way to cope was to take up a pair of secateurs and take it out on a few overgrown shrubs. Wise council indeed and Jim assures me that this works.

I guess that the secateurs were needed after the gas-stove incident.

Jim's mum wanted a new gas-stove so they decided to visit the show-room in Weymouth. For some unknown reason Jim's mum was already in town so his dad arranged to meet his wife at the bus-stop. Unfortunately they did not identify which of the two town bus stops was the rendezvous point and one was waiting at The Bridge whilst the other was waiting at The Statue.

Both working out what had gone wrong they each set off for the other bus-stop, one going down St Mary's Street and one going along St Thomas's Street. This meant that they did not meet on their brief journeys and when they got to their destinations the person they hoped to see was not there!

They did eventually meet up, by which time the Gas Showroom was closed and Jim's dad was in a temper which no doubt sent his mum into floods of tears.

However the next time they went, they went together and a gas-stove was duly bought.

The shrubs survived.

When Jim and his sister were both at school his mum went back to teaching as a private tutor to house-bound children whilst his dad always found something to occupy his hours out of the classroom.

Amongst his activities were repairing radios, house maintenance, servicing and mending his car, sweeping the chimney, crafting wonderful miniature furniture including two grand pianos, studying higher maths alongside his son and daughter, growing all the families vegetable needs, then in his retirement adding in teaching prisoners at Portland Jail, baking his own bread (the hard way, this was in the days before electric bread-makers).

In spite of leaving his sweet making to become a school teacher he never lost his skill and once the raw materials came off the war-time rationing he would be found in the kitchen making his favourite peppermint creams and nut toffee, whilst at Christmas he produce sugar mice and at Easter chocolate eggs.

As I said, Jim's dad was always occupied...you get the picture.

Jim is growing up and at holiday times and weekends we find him roaming free with his friends. These were not the days of parents worrying about what their children were getting up to, or at least not as long as they returned safely in time for lunch and for tea, so Jim was free to get up to whatever he chose to do. Sometimes, Jim admits, it is as well that his parents did not know what he was doing!

Several of Jim's mates had kites and Jim wanted one too.

No surprise that his dad set to and made him a large one with a lovingly crafted frame and a be-ribboned tail. The first time Jim took it out on a suitably windy day the kite flew brilliantly until a sudden downward gust saw it take a nose dive into a tree which obviously liked its new ornamentation. It kept hold of its unexpected guest in spite of the efforts to free it made by Jim and, later, Jim's upset dad.

It may be there still; Jim's dad made things to last!

Living near the sea meant Jim did plenty of messing around in boats and swimming, which his dad had taught him to do in the fast running tidal waters of The Fleet, where he had also taught his older pupils in the days pre-war when Risk Assessments were yet to be dreamed up.

The 1950's saw a craze for snorkelling as plastic ones came on the market. Jim decided to try this out for himself, but rather than spend money on the official equipment he fed a rubber tube through a tennis ball, the other end having a cotton reel and a piece of leather for the mouthpiece. You will not be surprised to learn that this did not work very well and a few mouthfuls of salty Portland Harbour soon saw the end of his underwater exploration.

Jim became a paper-boy and was up at six every morning except Sunday to cycle to the local distributer to pick up his bag. After making his own deliveries on a Saturday he joined a man who had a big round which on a weekday took him most of the morning. With Jim's help and company he was able to reduce the time taken and get home in time to catch the bus to watch a football or cricket match whilst Jim was happy to have some extra money in his purse.

During the war a bombing raid had missed the nearby army base where the Royal Engineers practised building pontoon bridges across the fast current of The Fleet, or 'Littlesea' as Jim always knew it.

One of the bombs fell harmlessly onto a footpath down to the beach. The resulting crater was impressively large and soon filled up with water, providing a welcome new home for frogs, toads, and their offspring, as well as crested newts. Jim and his mates passed many happy hours getting muddy, making dams, and trying to catch the newts in nets to see who could end up with the biggest one.

Jim thanks you Adolf; it was fun.

The Fleet lies between the glorious shingle of Chesil Beach and the coast of Dorset providing one of the finest views in the world when seen on a clear day from the top of the Isle of Portland.

During the war, besides training the troops in the art of temporary bridge building that would be needed once we invaded enemy territory, the Fleet was the testing site for the early prototypes of Barnes Wallis's 'bouncing bomb' which was to be used by 'The Dam Busters'.

I trust that the testing of the bombs and the bridge building were not taking place at the same time but there is a film of the trials with Chesil Beach clear in the background so for once I know for sure that Jim is not telling 'porkies'.

I mentioned the subject of frogs and their progeny a few lines back and I guess I need to not ignore the fact that all of creation, from plants and trees to the tiniest insects and even bacteria and viruses, have one driving force – to pass on their genes to the next generation.

It will hardly shock you then that from an early age Jim was well aware of his sexual drive.

He was once caught by his mother inspecting a girl of the same tender age as he in order to see where she differed from him. To her credit his mother took this in her stride and apart from giving him a lesson in 'The Facts of Life' accepted it as part of the growing up behaviour of most of us.

Jim's mum was a fan of the ukulele player and singer George Formby and some of his songs are by any definition somewhat more than suggestive. On reflection Jim thinks that his mum had more than a streak of naughtiness somewhere inside her.

This was in spite of her having a bad memory of an attempted assault on her when she was in her twenties. Thankfully she had managed to run off unharmed and no action was taken.

All Jim's sex education, such as it was, came from his mum and the fishmonger's daughter (Jim refuses to go into that).

His dad was far too Victorian to admit that such things went on.

Doctors and Nurses was a popular and probably harmless game played by children. Do they still do such things or has the easy availability of pornography on the internet rendered outdated such fairly innocent curiosity?

However it is hard to write a life story that ignores the fact that none of us would be here without sexual activity being pretty common. Fear not, I will try to be discrete and spare Jim's and your blushes.

Although Jim had several male friends he was then (and still is) always happiest in the company of the opposite sex. He enjoyed playing 'Hopscotch' and 'Statues', which was somewhat like the terrifying 'Weeping Angels' that Dr Who has to deal with.

With little traffic this took place on the road outside his house where they also played marbles in the gutters. The idea was to roll your marble to hit one's opponents marble and thus capture it.

However Jim and spherical objects were not comfortable in close proximity. This has remained true throughout his life. "Catch!" is always the precursor to some object hitting the deck. Don't even think about skittles!

His skill with marbles was no different so on at least one occasion he returned home in despair having lost every marble he owned to, of all things, a girl!

His future wife, Julia, still remembers having hysterics looking out of her upstairs classroom window watching Jim throw a tennis ball up and then trying to, and repeatedly failing to, hit it as it came back down.

Never mind getting it over the net; just to hit the ball would have been a triumph.

When it was the football season and the chosen captains had to pick their teams from the class Jim was always left to last and then put in goal where he could do least harm. Did he get cold though!

Maybe, as Barnes Wallace found, cylinders are better than spheres, though I cannot think of many sports that involve a cylinder unless one counts destroying dams with a bomb as a sport.

Sports may not have been his thing but his grandfather's business genes were active. A cousin gave Jim a set of Walt Disney glass slides and a magic lantern projector. Jim added to these some 35mm strips of stills from various movies and laid on film shows for local children at a one penny entrance fee. He still has the slides and the little battery operated projector somewhere in his house.

Perhaps they are now valuable antiques.

Then again, maybe not.

CHAPTER TEN

Jim Prepares For War

Not being taught 'How to pass the eleven-plus' did not prevent Jim and a few of his classmates from passing anyway and so, at just over eleven years old, Jim was kitted out with satchel, uniform and school cap (it was a punishable offence to be seen in school uniform without wearing a cap) and each day set off on his bicycle on the hilly route to Weymouth Grammar School. He usually cycled home for lunch and then returned for the afternoon.

It was a good few years later that Jim, whilst teaching his pupils how to dismantle and re-assemble their cycles, discovered that his bike, although having a three-speed hub gear, was 'close ratio' and more suited to cycling in Holland than in Dorset. No wonder then that those hills were a challenge although I am sure that it was good for his anatomy.

Nowadays, with multiple gears, it is a very rare sight to see a cyclist dismounted and pushing his bike up a hill. It seems they prefer to pedal furiously in bottom gear, though I am far from sure that this does not make the hill more exhausting as well as being slower than getting off and walking, especially as modern bikes are so much lighter than Jim's was.

Jim's mum had attended in the 1920's the same Grammar School as Jim was now attending. As you may recall she was the only one of her five siblings to be awarded a scholarship to go on to education after the age of fourteen. It was unusual then to have a mixed secondary school, although I imagine the boys and girls had separate play areas and were segregated in their class-rooms as well.

Even in Jim's time there was a separate playground for each and they generally still sat apart in the classrooms. However, clan-destine meetings were not impossible as Jim and his girlfriend found out towards the end of his schooldays. They were once discovered in a clinch round the back of the bike sheds by their headmaster who, as was his wont, asked them 'What are you doing?'

As if he didn't know!

However Jim's first year at Grammar School was not in the same building in which his mum had been educated. Instead, as the main school was over full, it was spent in a large house set in a landed-gentry type estate.

Jim enjoyed being there.

One highlight which he remembers well was the chemistry teacher demonstrating the explosive properties of some chem-ical substance. Chemistry was then, and remains still, some-what of a mystery to Jim; he is still bemused as to how an in-stant ice pack works just by hitting it. Whether understanding the cause or not he does remember a treacle-tin taking off with a large bang and hitting the ceiling.

Following behind Jim a few years later, Jim's sister remembers the same experiment so it seems that this was an annual event.

The ceiling must have been pretty robust.

As for the rest of his time there he remembers little of any note.

He used to help the dinner ladies with the washing up; goodness knows why, though maybe he got an iced lolly or something for his pains.

He upset his father by dropping the fob watch he had been given and breaking the balance staff. After the replacement fob watch suffered the same fate his dad realised that such Churchillian style watches and schoolboys do not make happy partners and he was given a Timex wrist watch. This was much more suitable and although a year or so later it stopped for a day, possibly due to altitude sickness, it soon recovered and stayed with Jim for many years with no more problems.

Pupils in 1953 fully expected to be 'called-up' on National Service so joining the school's Army Cadet Force seemed to Jim to be a sensible preparation for whatever he was called upon to do in defence of his country. He quite enjoyed the 'square bashing' and learning such useful skills as being able, in pitch blackness, to take to pieces and put back together a Bren gun.

As for his expertise actually firing a 'three-oh-three' rifle on the school's rifle range perhaps the least said the better. Maybe it is just as well he was never called upon to fire at anyone in anger. Perhaps he has inherited the genes of the unidentified archer who, as you may remember, managed to kill William Rufus in the New Forest when he claimed that he was aiming for a deer.

The cadet force always went on a week's training during the summer holidays and so at the tender age of twelve Jim found himself in an army camp on the North Devon coast. Those in charge were of the 'Let's make a man of you.' brigade so it was Reveille at 6 a.m. then cold showers and Physical Exercise followed by a cross country run and more cold showers.

Jim remembers his marching skills causing distress to a regular who was appointed to lead their square-bashing. Jim was told, in full-on volume army speak,

"You there!"

"Me, sergeant major?"

"Yes You! You march like a pregnant duck!"

One day the training was a mock battle. Jim survived for about as long as so many did going 'over the top' in the First World War. He spent nearly all of the day lying in the sandy dunes as he and his mates had been pronounced 'shot at and dead' soon after the exercise started.

None of this was to Jim's taste, being as you know more 'one of the girls' than 'one of the boys' but he survived the experience if not the mock-battle.

What should have been an enormous treat was a flight from a nearby airfield in a two-seater plane. The preparation for this involved being fitted with a very heavy adult-size parachute which rendered Jim almost unable to stand.

The two seater plane took two cadets up at a time and I expect you can work out that there was only one spare seat as it seemed advisable to let the pilot have the other one. Jim was the one chosen to sit on the floor of the plane behind the seats from which position he could see nothing.

To put it mildly his first flight was far from memorable, although his second, many years later, would prove more exciting.

To add to his woes, when he struggled back off the plane after (he presumes, though he has no evidence) being up in the air and landing again, he found his Timex watch had stopped. He complained about this to an officer who, I am sure correctly, told him that watches were not affected by altitude. I guess it might have been the severe vibration Jim experienced whilst sitting on the floor of the plane that affected the watch and it did start up again a while later.

However Jim's main memory of this first taste of army life was one evening when as a treat they were given a film show in a large marquee. The main feature was Rudyard Kipling's 'Kim' which I guess was a reasonable choice if you know the story.

Someone decided that it would be good to start the presentation with graphic film of the British Army's 1945 entry into Belson, the Nazi concentration/extermination camp.

Showing this to a sensitive twelve-year-old, with its scenes of English troops using bulldozers to collect hundreds of naked rotting dead bodies for a mass grave, left an indelible image in Jim's brain.

If you find this seemingly callous use of a bulldozer hard to believe you can find the film shot at the time on the internet but I would not advise it.

Later in Jim's life one of his colleagues had been amongst the British troops who were the first into Belson and he, hardly surprisingly, was traumatised by the experience to the day he died.

That humans can do the appalling things that the Nazis did in Jim's early days makes him almost ashamed to admit that he too is a human being. He wonders though if he himself would have been capable of such monstrous cruelty if the Germans had successfully invaded Britain and he had grown up with a Nazi education.

Hardly on a par with such a terrible way to treat people, but cruel all the same, was one of the games played by the tougher boys when they crept up to a sleeping cadet and put his hand into a bowl of water. This was supposed to make the victim 'wet the bed', if calling a straw-filled sack on a duckboard can justifiably be described as 'a bed'. Fortunately they spared Jim being either one of the instigators or, as far as he knows, the victim, and Jim has no idea if their unkind game was ever successful.

Jim was spared the next year's week of 'toughening up' as the day before he was due to catch the train his torso came out in painful huge red lacerations looking as if he had been whipped, facing the wrong way, and to within inches of his life.

His horrified mum summoned the doctor.

For your benefit, if you are somewhat younger than Jim and me, in those days more often than not the doctor came to the patient, not like now when if feeling unwell you have to drag yourself out of your sick-bed to go to the surgery or else dial 111 and see if they think you are ill enough for an ambulance to be called.

Anyway, as I was saying, the doctor came and was as horrified as Jim's mum. He did not have a clue what it was that had caused the wounds and in those days 'Googling' the symptoms was only a writer's fantasy during a 'Journey into Space' episode on the radio. He advised that Jim should be kept in isolation and certainly should not go to cadet camp.

'Thank you Lord.' thought Jim, who was quite devout in those days, complete with a crucifix on his bedroom wall.

Looking back now it seems highly likely that Jim had swum into the tentacles of a 'Portuguese Man of War', a particularly vicious jelly-fish that, in warm weather and with the wind in the right direction, would sometimes find its way into Portland Harbour. It can, though rarely does, kill a human and it seems that Jim was not wanted up there yet; the pain eased, and after a few days Jim recovered.

Later cadet 'holidays' were less painful and therefore less memorable and Jim found that he enjoyed laying telephone cables and using the early versions of i-phones, then known as portable short-wave radios, though 'portable' is a questionable description of something that was brick-sized and at least twice as heavy.

However his experience of life in the army in the 1950's did nothing to make Jim look forward to National Service. How he would have enjoyed the two years or, more likely, not have enjoyed the two years, we shall never know as the government closed the activity down three months before Jim was due to be called to the flag.

CHAPTER ELEVEN

Escaped Gran

I mentioned Charles Chiltern's 'Journey Into Space' a few lines back. This was a much enjoyed, if somewhat frightening, serial on the radio. It starred Jet Morgan as an astronaut.

Jim's parents did not have a television while Jim was growing up so the radio and books were the only entertainments available. This may have been a good thing as radio plays give more scope to the listener's imagination than television does.

The 'behind the sofa' watching, or rather avoiding watching, of Dr Who was not something that Jim would experience, if that ever really happens and is not just an urban myth. However Jim can still remember the shock of someone, or some thing, knocking on the outside of Jet Morgan's space ship. I guess modern day cosmonauts would feel the same way that Jet Morgan, and Jim, did if they heard the same urgent rapping.

The aforesaid urgent rapping cued the closing dramatic music. Jim would have to tune in again the following week to find out who, or what, was trying to make contact.

Thanks to the miracle of the internet, you too can listen to some of the episodes on line.

Prepare to be terrified!

As Jim grew older he was allowed to stay up later than usual at the weekends and one treat was to listen to 'At the Luscombes' on the radio at 7:40 pm on a Saturday. This was a hugely successful story of West Country folk and ran for more than a thousand episodes from 1948 to 1964. Then from 1953 on a Friday there was 'Friday Night is Music Night' which Jim's family enjoyed.

This has been even longer running than 'The Luscombes' as it is broadcast to this day, if you can tear yourself away from the television or your smart phone, though it is now 'Sunday Night is Music Night' so don't try to tune into it on a Friday.

Jim's gran's sister, known to him as 'Aunt Eliza', came to live with the family in her old age. Very old – she nearly made 100 and almost certainly would have done if she had not fallen in her late nineties when she lost her balance while picking up a piece of litter on the pavement and broke her hip. Like Jim's great-grandmother in Portsmouth. who you may recall suffered the same injury, Aunt Eliza never really recovered.

Where was I? Oh yes, Aunt Eliza was a great fan of The Archers, another huge long-runner although I am sure Jim's aunt would have been shocked at recent storylines.

She also never missed Mrs Dale's Diary. Mrs Dale's husband was a doctor and was also a Jim. A favourite line to introduce some problem that Dr Jim was about to run into was 'I'm rather worried about Jim.' which perhaps not surprisingly was uttered more than a few times by our Jim's mum.

And yes, there is the quote in Wikipedia!

The next few years at the main school were happily fairly incident free for Jim apart from more trouble involving fish.

At home he again showed some of his grandfather's business acumen by his various projects to make useful pocket money.

He learnt conjuring tricks, though depending on props rather than sleight-of-hand, and so entertained children at parties in return for a small fee. His piano playing had improved enough to perform for a few local clubs. He upgraded from his magic lantern, buying a 9.5 mm film projector and hiring black and white silent films featuring such greats as Charlie Chaplin and Laurel and Hardy, as well as thrillers like The Cabinet of Dr Caligari. He showed the films at his youth club and at birthday parties, again in return for a small fee.

Much of the funds brought in from these activities were invested in used stamps, a collection which he still has; I wonder if it has increased in value?

He also bought extra track for his 'O' gauge clockwork railway. Although he craved an electric Dublo ('OO' gauge; get it?) train set he never managed to be able to afford that and I think he has grown out of that urge at last although he still loves trains.

Other hobbies, this time not for profit, were building engineering masterpieces with his Meccano set. The additional pieces to make his kit up to the next number in the sequence were a regular Christmas gift from his Nannie and Pa. He reached Set Eight but sadly he never made it to the final goal of the mighty Number Ten.

He loved making intricate miniature card models, called 'Micromodels', which scaled HMS Victory, Windsor Castle, the Houses of Parliament and so on down to a model no bigger than a spread out hand.

You will gather than Jim, like his dad, was never lost for something to do.

When he was fifteen Jim was left in the house with his Gran, by now experiencing full blown dementia. This even included accusing Jim's saintly sister of stealing money from her when in fact Gran had put what money she had somewhere other than where she expected it to be.

I guess if you have reached Jim's age of three score years and twenty you will know the feeling!

One day Jim's parents went shopping and left Jim as Gran's

keeper. The main door was secured with a bolt at the top of it, well out of Gran's reach. The back-door was locked with a key which Jim had in his pocket. What could possibly go wrong? Time to practise a Mozart piano sonata, or perhaps two.

Some way through one of these glorious pieces of music there came a knock on the front door.

"Did you know that your Gran is half a mile away on the way to Portland, with her nightie tucked into her pants, … and in her slippers?"

Of course Jim did not know! What a stupid question.

Anyway Jim was not sure which was the most vital fact out of these three shocking pieces of information. I guess in total it came down to the horror that his Gran had somehow escaped. How come? The chair by the front door was the major clue, not needing Sherlock Holmes to unravel the mystery of her break for freedom.

Jim set off to search for his Gran. An old lady with her nightie tucked into her knickers, AND in her slippers of all things, was not hard to spot and Gran allowed Jim to walk her back home, where her mum and dad would be waiting to greet her!

Unfortunately the neighbourhood watch witnessed Jim's return with his Gran on his arm and split to Jim's mother when she returned home.

Jim blamed Mozart, who could neither deny nor admit his part but Wolfgang and Jim were soon forgiven and, as I have said at least once before, it was a crime that taught Jim a lesson and yet another that was only committed once in his life. Lots more different ones ahead I fear.

No wonder that this book is called Jim Jams.

CHAPTER TWELVE

Man Up The Pole

Gran died peacefully in her bed some months later.

Why do so many of us fear our own death when most people manage it as easily as falling asleep whilst sat in an arm-chair watching TV? And yes, Jim does that frequently, although to date he has always woken up this side of the grave, even if somewhat confused as to where he is and why.

In one of those strange coincidences that Charles Dicken's so loved, Gran, during her last day lying on her death bed, told Jim's mum that there was a man at the top of the telegraph-pole that she could see out of the window. There wasn't of course.

Well there was, but that was the day after and Gran was dead by then.

Is seeing a man up a pole, in a future yet to come, a sign of imminent death? Possibly. Who knows?

As was the norm in those days, Gran was left on display in her bedroom, neatly laid-out in her coffin.

Jim never told his parents but curiosity got the better of him and before the coffin lid was screwed down he took one last look at his Gran, by then somewhat the worse for wear, which served him right I guess. We know that Egyptian mummies deteriorate to some extent and I expect even Lenin needed the occasional application of Polyfilla.

Jim was to get a personal view of a dead body three more times in his life but that is for later. You will have to wait for the details.

Jim's family could not afford what is now regarded as a 'proper' holiday and the nearest he came to foreign travel was a day trip on the 'tomato boat' to Guernsey.

Sadly all he saw of the island, which is of course not 'foreign' anyway, was a café on the dockside as when the ship was half way across the English Channel the fog descended. Although the captain pressed on hopefully towards the Channel Islands he had to reduce speed and then was unable to safely enter the destination port for some hours so that half-an-hour after managing to dock it was time to leave and return to Weymouth. As they were deck passengers it was unmemorable except for how cold and damp Jim and his family became on the journey.

Rather more successful was a trip on the paddle steamer Consul from Weymouth to Lulworth Cove. Only seven miles so hardly a round the world cruise but an adventure all the same and there was no fog that day.

Come fog, rain or shine, weather problems did not affect Jim's regular trips to Hampshire in the summer holidays, staying either with his Aunt Lily, his mum's sister who I mentioned when I was telling you of Jim's dad's proposal, or with his dad's sister and his grandparents, Nannie and Pa, on their smallholding.

Jim caught the train from Weymouth to Southampton which he loved doing. It was usually powered by a streamlined Merchant Navy Class steam engine in bright green livery and Jim always walked to the front of the train to admire it before it set off for London.

For his seventy-fifth birthday treat his daughter gave him a day joining the volunteers running a local steam line and so he got to drive an engine, which he had longed to do all his life; unfortunately it was not Merchant Navy Class.

Coming back to his catching a train as a teenager, the worry for

Jim was that he would miss the stop at Southampton and find himself at Basingstoke, Hook, or even Waterloo. There were no announcements on the train as nowadays so it was a case of looking at every stop for a platform sign telling you where you were. However Jim soon learnt the names of every station on the line and managed to avoid a disastrous mistake, well it seemed to him that it would be disastrous, worry pot that he was (and still is).

Holidays with Auntie Vi, Nannie and Pa were always a treat. They had things that Jim did not have at home, like a car, their own telephone, a freezer, and a television (black and white) which was watched avidly every evening (BBC – not much choice really!) whilst supper was eaten on laps.

Auntie Vi was a superb pianist and Jim was in awe of her ability to listen to a tune and immediately play it herself. To hear her play Ragtime was miraculous to Jim, whose pianistic ability was then, and I fear still is, way below that of his aunt.

One of his jobs each summer was to steer an Allen Scythe around the apple trees in the orchard. He loved doing this although the scythe, petrol-engine driven and difficult to steer, with open blades at the front, could well have removed his toes, his fingers, or possibly larger items that he would find useful in his later life. Health and Safety was not a consideration in those days.

One year he had an Easter Holiday there and he was given the job of pollinating with a small soft paint brush a peach tree that had been trained over the side of the bungalow. Sadly one of his first experiences of what 'the birds and the bees' was all about was not successful and to his everlasting shame he was told on the next visit that his efforts to produce some fruit had been a complete failure.

Given that any helpful bees must have also failed in their service, probably due to a late frost, maybe his reproductive efforts were not so bad. Jim always thought of that peach tree when in his dotage he was pollinating, or maybe we should say trying to pollinate, his own 'minarette' apple and pear trees.

Much later on Jim tried to grow his own fan-trained peach tree. It survived for several years, only fruited once, and Jim knew when he was beaten. The climate won out as this was in the days before 'global warming' became an all too real problem.

You may have noticed that I wrote 'one of his first' in the last but two paragraphs. I'll say no more; just remind you of the fishmonger's daughter in Chapter Nine!

Closer to home Jim also helped his dad on the garden and allotment, learning many useful skills.

On one occasion he was given the job of clearing from a patch of the back garden the couch grass that had become a severe problem. If you know anything about couch grass you will know that its white roots spread throughout the soil and if you leave a tiny bit behind the grass soon enthusiastically repopulates the area. Jim's dad was not good at praising his son, or so Jim thought, but he was told some years later that he must have done an excellent job on removing all the roots as the couch grass had never returned.

Such praise was to be treasured.

However that does not mean that he and his dad did not get on, far from it, and he was taught much useful DIY. Besides gardening he learnt electrical rewiring, plumbing, painting, wood and metal working, book-binding, care of a car and so on.

One summer Jim and his dad repointed the whole end brick-wall of their two story house, perched together on a plank between two ladders.

As with his time behind the Allen Scythe, maybe Jim was lucky to survive into adulthood.

CHAPTER THIRTEEN

More Living Dangerously

In 1955 Jim's dad, with Rosemary no longer a drain on his resources, bought a car. He had owned a motorbike and a car as a youth and had taught himself to drive, as one could before driving tests started in 1934.

When Jim's mum announced that she wanted to learn to drive his dad decided to teach her himself. I guess, knowing of Jim's dad's usual philosophy, that does not surprise you.

However, perhaps never having had a lesson himself (something that as we shall see later was also to be true of Jim) it turned out that, whilst he was excellent as a classroom teacher, he was not so good as a driving instructor in the passenger seat where he was in danger of losing life or limb.

This was long before the introduction of seat belts and air-bags.

On their first drive Jim's dad, trying to keep his wife away from other traffic (not that there was very much of that in the fifties) decided to start her driving experience in a narrow country lane. Not ideal when one is still trying to remember which foot operates which pedal let alone having to steer as well. Perhaps it is no surprise that the car came to grief in a hedge. Not much damage to the hedge or the car but his mum came home in tears.

A few weeks later, not having had any more accidents, Jim's mum was considered competent enough to take the wheel on the road to Southampton with Jim and his sister in the back. They reached Wool level-crossing which is on the main line from Weymouth to Southampton.

The gates were open so it was safe to cross the lines.

Unfortunately, half way over Florrie stalled the car, which was not so safe. A level crossing was not an ideal place to stall a vehicle; it still isn't but it was especially dangerous in those days before all the modern electronics and communications came in.

Jim's mum panicked.

Jim's dad panicked.

Jim and his sister panicked.

Jim's dad got out and rushed to the driver's door and his mum moved to the passenger seat. His dad got the engine going again and they safely left the crossing.

Whew!!

More tears and Jim's mum's confidence was utterly shattered.

Jim thinks that this was the end of his dad's attempt to teach his wife to drive.

It was not the end of her driving experience though as a short while later came the 1956 'Suez Crisis', one result of which was that petrol went on ration.

The government, in one of those somewhat inexplicable decisions that politicians seem wont to make, put the issuing and supervising of petrol rationing into the hands of the driving-test examiners. That meant driving tests were not held and the government overcame this by allowing new drivers to take to the wheel without anyone beside them to advise them, or in Jim's mum's case to drive them to tears.

I know it is hard to believe any politician could come up with such bizarre decisions.

Although, on second thoughts, maybe you think that it is not so hard to believe.

Anyway Jim suggested that he went out in the car with his mum to see if he could restore her confidence, although his own experience was limited to a pedal cycle and the bumper cars at the annual November Portland Fair.

His mum thought it was worth a try, so it was agreed.

Jim proved more patient than his dad. He was also less terrified; after all he was a teenager.

He was immortal!

Soon his mum was able to make short journeys on her own and when driving tests came back a couple of years later she passed first time.

Let's return to the subject of fishes.

Jim had by now started to learn to play the church organ.

His piano teacher, Miss Galpin Atwool (what a glorious name!) was also an organist, so every Sunday afternoon she joined Jim in the church for his lesson.

To understand where this is going you need to know of his Uncle Bill, a craft teacher and very keen fisherman. He lived within sight of the church tower and thought it would be much improved with a weathervane at the top.

Uncle Bill kept Jim's family supplied with fish all through the war, and long after, right up to a few weeks before he died (from pneumonia, which seemed rough justice when his avowed cure-all was to strip off and sit on Chesil Beach. Maybe he tempted the gods once too often).

Of course, being an obsessive angler, the ornament was to be a fish, made with great skill out of beaten copper with NESW arms on the spindle. (Writing NESW reminds me that my pupils used to remember this as 'Never Eat Shredded Wheat', which probably would not best please the Nestle company!)

The new feature was named 'The Weatherfish'. To be visible at the top of quite a tall tower it had to be large, and large it was, nearly two metres (or in those days six feet) high and wide.

Jim was given the job of helping his uncle install the addition to the tower's beauty.

Firstly they hauled up the weatherfish on a long rope (or perhaps it was a fishing line; Jim forgets which). This was followed by buckets of cement to fix it into the top of the tower.

Once this was accomplished the good folk of the area were no longer left in any doubt as to the direction of the wind, assuming it was not already obvious to them as soon as they stepped out of their front doors.

Unfortunately (you knew there had to be an unfortunately) one Sunday afternoon Jim had left the church after his organ lesson and was setting off for home when the skies went black, heavy rain fell, and there was an enormous flash and simultaneously an equally enormous bang.

If you know your science you will know that light travels much faster than sound, which is why usually the flash of lightning arrives before the crash of thunder, proving that the electrical discharge is some long distance away.

If they happen at the same time it is not good news!

Jim was unharmed although he was lucky as the next day he learnt that the church tower had been struck by a thunderbolt, shaking the building to its foundations and bringing down the dust, if not the rock, of ages onto the pews, altar, hymn books and so on.

If Jim and Miss Galpin Atwool had still been at the organ I guess they too would have been more than a little shaken and dusty. They escaped a nasty shock by minutes.

Most towers have a metal spike and a thick wire running down to the earth below, hence the term 'lightning conductor'. I guess Jim's church tower was no different but, as the tower being struck by lightning was a first, as far as anyone could recall, the church council decided, rightly or wrongly (only God knows) that the lightning had been attracted by the new weatherfish.

It would have to be removed forthwith or sooner.

Jim's uncle was deeply offended by the suggestion that he was responsible for the church being put in peril of collapse and refused to take his pride and joy off the tower.

However, taken off it had to be and a local builder was called in to remove the offending item whether it was innocent or guilty.

Uncle Bill never attended the church again until his funeral, when he was given no choice.

This was not Jim's only close encounter with Thor, or possibly Zeus, letting his thunderbolts loose on the world as many years later the chimney of a neighbour's house in his terrace was struck while Jim and his wife were having breakfast. They had a skylight in the kitchen ceiling and a split second after the deafening crash they saw red hot pieces of brick flying over their heads.

Jim rushed to his neighbours to see if they were OK, which they were, but there was water dripping through their landing ceiling.

On going into their loft to check the damage he found a melted water pipe and a small area of burnt wood. That there was no major conflagration was due to good fortune, the water leaking from the melted pipe having put out the fire.

The local fire brigade therefore had no need of their hoses although they had fun on the roof removing what was left of the wrecked chimney. Other houses in the area had damage to their electrics, their central heating systems, and their telephones.

A lightning strike is no small event.

CHAPTER FOURTEEN

The Great Flood

While we are on the subject of fishes (the weatherfish that is) let's learn about a much smaller member of the family that caused Jim to be involved in another minor disaster.

Biology was always a favourite subject for Jim; this was not hindered by his adoration of the young biology teacher, Miss Fowler.

Jim decided that he would impress his idolized teacher by keeping sticklebacks. These are very small fish that need circulating fresh water if they are to survive in captivity. Or so he was told.

His solution to the problem of running water was to connect a glass tank to the cold water tap in the biology lab, making an s-bend in a glass tube emptying into the sink which kept the level of water in the aquarium stable.

This worked well for several weeks. The sticklebacks were happy and so was Jim as his teacher was mightily impressed.

Came half-term week and at the end of it Jim returned to school to check whether his fish had survived without their daily diet of chopped up worms, only to be met at the 'bilge-lab' door by his teacher who was in deep trouble.

You can read into 'deep' one of two possible meanings.

It seems that over half-term a cleaner, needing the tap, had disconnected the tube from it to the aquarium, re-connecting it when she had finished her work. She did not know that Jim's apparatus relied on a very low amount of water flowing from the mains supply and unfortunately she left the tap far too open.

The result was a flooded room, the water coming through the

ceiling of the female staffroom below and flooding that as well.

Quite why Jim did not get into serious trouble over this remains a mystery to him to this day. Maybe his teacher took the blame and, in all fairness, it is forgivable (just) that someone altering his carefully balanced hydraulic system was not an anticipated event.

Jim started a Field Club which held weekly meetings and trips out to the country at weekends. He also started his publishing career by producing a duplicated magazine.

Jim tells me that these are now collector's items (deluded or what?) but I think the following piece is worthy of your attention. It was occasioned by his teacher, the adored Miss Fowler, asking her pupils to bring in some frogs for dissection.

Frogs

Bring us some frogs went out the plea

Which started all our misery.

Before another week had passed

The frogs turned up, extremely fast.

Aquariums were soon complete

With rocks and stones and worms for meat.

Miss Fowler came with hasty tread

But in a voice of horror said

"Those all are toads, not one a frog!"

An air of gloom, like London smog,

Fell over all the company,

But Mr Daniel said "You'll see;
They are the same internally."

Soon the smell of toads dissected
All the school with stink infected.
If someone followed on the trail
They found the smell of toad entrail
Was strongest near the Bilge Lab door
Where if they entered, on the floor
Lay crimson pools of toady gore.

And if they glanced around the room
Found everywhere an air of gloom,
Whilst in one corner was a fire,
Miss Fowler on the funeral pyre
Burnt up the maimed remains of life
Butchered by cruel dissecting knife.

In ev'ry year the plea's renewed
Amphibian insides are viewed.
Help us stop this persecution!
Change the British Constitution!
Hey you! Don't join the gathering.
Leave the frogs and toads to spawning.

I have mentioned Jim's life-long love of performing in front of people, which had not gone unnoticed by his teachers, so he was cast in the lead role in 'Tobias and the Angel'. He was Tobias.

I don't think he would have made a convincing angel!

The play is based on the story in the Apocrypha. It also involves a large fish (though no lightning and thunder, or flooded schools). I will leave you to look it up in your copy of the Apocrypha (or use your smart phone).

Jim enjoyed acting the part although the role involved learning many long passages and the two performances did not go entirely to plan as he was later told by the Physics teacher, who produced school plays as a side-line.

Apparently the first evening Tobias cut quite a chunk out of the play as written by James Brodie and on the second he did one speech twice!

The next year they did 'The Town That Would Have a Pageant' and Jim played the town clerk. He had no long speeches so the performances were as the author intended.

The school had a tradition of the sixth-form pupils putting on a Gilbert and Sullivan Operetta each year. This had begun when his mum was at the same school.

The team of teachers who produced the performances thought that, with his known acting credentials, Jim would be cast in a leading role, but when he auditioned they were taken aback by his inability to sing in tune now that his voice had broken. Although he was given two chances to sing melodiously he failed and they relegated him to the chorus line.

I fear Jim's ability to sing melodiously has not improved with the passing of the years. If you happen to find yourself next to him in church some day I would advise you to move at the first opportunity.

Coincidentally Jim's mum had been in the chorus of the same operetta, 'The Mikado', way back in 1920. So it was as a Japanese nobleman and as a sailor fair in 'H.M.S. Pinafore' that saw him on the stage for the next two years.

This brought his 'official' acting career to an end, though Jim feels that with his teaching in school and his volunteering in the Red Cross he has continued to act all his life.

One of his performances many years later in a first-aid class proved all too realistic when he was acting out having a cardiac arrest and was more than a little discomforted to find his chest suddenly being energetically pumped up and down in an effort to keep him alive.

This is quite likely to fracture ribs and cause internal injuries and so is not recommended for someone whose heart is working normally, which is why first-aiders are taught to check the casualty for breathing before starting the procedure.

Jim's would-be 'saviour' seems to have been lost in dreamland during this part of the training.

Not surprisingly Jim very soon 'recovered' consciousness and stopped the over-enthusiastic first-aider, fortunately before any damage was done.

I have digressed (again) haven't I. Sorry!

At the end of five years in a Grammar School all pupils took their General Certificate of Education exams, usually in eight subjects. Candidates were told the mark awarded and either passed, if they gained more than about 47%, or failed. There were no grades as now.

Jim managed six passes.

Not entirely to his surprise he failed to pass French and Chemistry, though both these were close to a pass mark.

Learning a foreign language is not something Jim has ever had success with and it was particularly hard in those days when it was mainly taught from text books of grammar.

Looking back he realises that he did not fully comprehend that people actually spoke French 'over the garden fence' in that never seen country across the English Channel.

Chemistry also made little sense to Jim, not helped by the teacher seeming more than a little eccentric and, together with the female French teacher, somewhat terrifying.

Both these failures had a big influence on Jim's future path in life which would not have been the case with most of the six he did get. Without a foreign language a student could not go to University; without Chemistry Jim was not allowed to take Biology 'A' levels so ending his time in Miss Fowler's company.

He re-took Chemistry once and French twice. All three efforts had much the same result so he gave up and settled down to his chosen three 'A' levels of Pure Maths, Applied Maths, and Physics.

Jim, somewhat to the surprise of his teachers, managed to pass all these and was then accepted at St Luke's Training College in Exeter, intending to become a Junior School teacher.

Not quite how it worked out as you will see.

However before I pass on to that stage in Jim's life I fear we must return to the subject of hormones, testosterone being the one we need to address.

CHAPTER FIFTEEN

In Which Jim Goes A-Courting

Jim's first foray into 'courting' was when he was sixteen.

He arranged to go to 'the pictures' (cinema) with Elizabeth who went to the same youth club as him.

As usual in those days there was a double feature, 'Rock Around the Clock' and the comedy 'Doctor at Sea'.

Strange bedfellows I guess.

In those days there was no fixed time to go in so customers were were coming and going all through the films.

Elizabeth and Jim caught the bus into town and arrived at the cinema in the early evening half-way through the comedy feature. After a few hours the film got to the point at which they had come in but, as they were enjoying it so much, they stayed another hour to watch it through to its end.

Coming out of the cinema they decided to walk home along the cliff path.

Jim does not remember whose decision this was and has wondered since if Elizabeth was expecting more than a walk, though he was far too nervous to initiate anything other than putting one foot in front of the other.

Elizabeth was escorted unmolested back to her home without even a goodnight kiss.

By the time Jim reached home it was quite late and his parents were frantic, imagining some disaster had befallen their son, or maybe thought that he had indeed been 'Rolling in the Clover' with his female companion.

Was he in trouble? Was he just!

It was some time before he dared again take out a young lady.

Perhaps adding to their concern, a few days later Jim bought the record of 'Rock Around the Clock' by Bill Hayley and the Comets.

This horrified his father for whom any 'music' written much later than when Beethoven's ink was still wet on the page was far too avant garde.

A year or so passes and we come to the Christmas examinations during Jim's first 'A' levels year in the 'Sixth Form'.

Jim has always set a high standard for himself and suffers from depression when, as all too often happens, he fails to attain the standard he expects.

One of his class-mates somehow got to see the marks the Physics candidates had been awarded and told Jim he had done badly.

Jim could not cope with this news and instead of going home at lunch-time he went to sit in the local church where he was spotted some hours later by the organist who set off to tell Jim's parents.

By this time they were fearing the worst. They had contacted the school who could not explain Jim's disappearance and they had come close to reporting him to the police as a missing person.

The news from the organist that Jim was sitting quietly in the church was a huge relief to them and his dad set off to collect his son.

The doctor was summoned and 'depression' diagnosed.

The school decided that Jim must have been bullied and delivered a strong rebuke to his peers. This was not the case but as it turns out it was a fortunate mis-diagnosis.

Why was that?

Well, Jim had already spotted Julia, a girl in the next year up, while they were both studying in the school library.

He took a strong fancy to her. Blame the genes.

A few days after he returned to school in early January, finding that his Physics results weren't that terrible anyway, he plucked up the courage to ask Julia if she would like to come to a symphony concert at the weekend.

Although she was 'seeing' another boy she felt sorry for Jim who had been suffering, she presumed, from the effects of the (imaginary) bullying and she said that she would.

On the way back to the bus-stop after the concert Jim found himself passionately kissing his companion.

Whether it was the effect of the music or the moonlight he is not sure.

As I have already told you Jim did not understand 'Chemistry' yet it seems the chemistry between the two of them had a positive reaction and they soon started 'courting' in earnest.

Jim was invited to tea at Julia's parents' house and managed to impress Julia's mum with his good manners so had her blessing in continuing to take out her only daughter.

Jim, like his dad, is both impulsive and persistent.

Julia was bowled along in an increasingly intimate relationship as the year went on, though don't read too much into that.

We are only at the beginning of 'The Swinging Sixties'. Birth control pills were still only just becoming available, prescribed by a doctor only for a married couple with a good reason for needing 'the pill'. The 'morning after' pill was still a fantasy. 'Johnnies' were not on public display as they are nowadays and only available from a chemist or possibly a barber ("Something for the weekend, sir?"). Abortion was illegal except for medical reasons.

◆ ◆ ◆

Jim's first sixth-form year has come to a close and it is the summer holidays.

Julia, being in the year above though only ten months older, is moving to Exmouth to train as a teacher. She had wanted to train as a nurse but was not accepted, goodness knows why not; she would have been a brilliant one, caring and efficient.

However, as many an ex-pupil will avow, she instead became a much loved and excellent teacher. What the sick lost out on, the healthy future citizens of the United Kingdom gained.

Jim had a distant relation who was the boss of the Weymouth Southern National bus company and Jim was taken on as a conductor for the holiday season.

In those days the driver was in a separate cab, responsible for steering the vehicle safely to its destination whilst the conductor looked after passengers, taking their fares and helping strangers get off at the right stops. The driver and his mate kept in touch with an electric bell, which in its simplest form was one ring for stop at the next bus-stop and two rings for pull away or keep going.

The conductor was also in charge of the time-keeping, a fact which obviously Jim was not fully briefed on, or maybe like the first-aid trainee who later tried to perform real CPR on him, he failed to pay this matter sufficient attention during his training.

Jim was paired with Bob, a much older driver, and they got on really well together, developing the bell system into a complexity almost rivalling the Morse code and around the town this worked well.

The second week together they were given the long run to Axminster where passengers changed buses to the Devon line and went on to Exeter. On the way back there were few passengers when they left Axminster and those aboard were all heading for Weymouth.

With no-one waiting at the bus stops Jim used his developed bell system to let Bob know that he could keep on going, rather forgetting that he was supposed to be making sure the service kept to the timetable.

In a town this would not matter as there would soon be 'another one behind' but this country route was only one every two hours, so keeping to the timetable was crucial.

As the journey went on it is obvious, with hindsight, that the reason for the empty bus-stops was that the bus had already gone through quite a long time ahead of its appointed time.

Passengers were left waiting at their stop for a bus that was already well on its way back to Weymouth.

When Jim and Bob arrived back (nice and early) at the bus station they were met by a very angry boss who marched Bob off to his office.

Several potential passengers had phoned the station to enquire why their bus was so late and he had paid out for several taxis to take them to their destination.

Poor dear Bob. It really was Jim's fault, not his, but he got it in the ear and perhaps he should have realised the serious mistake his rookie conductor was making.

Jim's bus conducting days could have ended almost as soon as they began.

Fortunately blood is thicker than water so he was forgiven by his distant relation, though probably not by Bob who was given a new partner; one who kept an eye on both his watch and the timetable.

Jim would not make that mistake again.

Have I said that before?

Jim continued working on the buses all hours God gave him, and some he didn't, throughout every holiday for the next three years. He recalls it as being a most enjoyable time.

In the summer many families from the Midlands, particularly from Birmingham, came for their annual works' holidays and they were always good fun. He especially enjoyed the Portland Bill run, when he became a tour guide, giving the holidaymakers the history of the sights they were enjoying.

Sometimes he got a tip at the destination!

The only worry, and you know how Jim worries, came at the end of the day when the ticket printing machine indicated how much cash you should have in your bag. If you had too little you had to make it up from your wages.

This I guess was fair enough but it was all too easy to forget that one had turned the 'shillings' lever on and hence repeatedly issue, for example, a 'One shilling and sixpence' ticket (1/6) for a sixpenny fare. Do this too often and you could be many pounds wrong before you noticed your error.

Jim only made the mistake once.

Not again?

Oh yes!

Like his first bus conducting disaster he was forgiven and it was accepted that what he had in his bag was the correct amount.

Jim's bus company boss was fortunately not only a distant relative but also a very soft-hearted man and none the worse for that.

Julia found holiday jobs too, one year making candy-floss on Weymouth beach, and in another being a silver-service waitress at a very up-market Portland hotel.

Let's rewind a little to Jim's last year as a pupil and the start of his role at the front of the classroom. During Julia's first year at Exmouth, Jim wrote to her very many times, almost daily; long passionate letters, filled with outpourings of love for her.

Like Byron's diaries (though this is their only common ground) they went up in flames a year or two later, but on a bonfire in the garden rather than in the fireplace of John Murray's publishing house.

Coincidentally, much later in his life, Jim was often within touching distance of the said fireplace.

Maybe Jim should have been studying rather than writing love letters, though somehow he kept up with his schoolwork at the same time.

Besotted he certainly was and he never looked at another girl, although one day Irene ('Alice in Wonderland', see Chapter Six) got on his bus with a friend and they had a long chat. He was too in love with Julia to ask Irene out, though he did give her a free ride which could have cost him his job and yet another disaster if an Inspector had boarded the bus.

Sometimes Jim gets away with it!

He applied to study music and maths at Saint Luke's Church of England Teacher Training College in Exeter, just a few miles from his beloved Julia in Exmouth.

Lady Fortune smiled on him.

The mathematics intake was over-subscribed and, as his teachers doubted that he would do well at 'A' level, the omens were not good.

Luckily there were very few applications to study music that year so he was given a college place with music as his main subject even though he had no qualifications except Grade Five piano.

Fortunately he was not asked to sing at his interview!

As it turned out he passed his three 'A' levels reasonably well, proving his teacher's doubts unjustified, and the next September saw him leaving home and starting his two year training at St Luke's.

Hold on a minute. Before he leaves school as a pupil Jim must plead guilty to a prank.

It had been the tradition for many years for the leaving pupils to come up with ideas to celebrate their final day minus one. Such silly japes as a whitewash notice under the headmaster's window 'Beware. This beast bites!' or a pair of bloomers flying from the roof. You get the idea.

The teachers were fed up with this nonsense and the headmaster issued a stern warning that any incursions onto school property on the evening of the penultimate day would be regarded as a trespass and a serious breach of the rules.

Anyone caught on the premises would be suspended. On reflection this seems hardly a sensible punishment seeing as the offender would be leaving the same day.

Jim and his fellow leavers decided to go ahead with their plans anyway and met up in the dark in the wild area adjoining the rear of the school.

However the teaching staff were seen to be on guard so the criminals did not enter the school at the planned zero hour. When the teachers, after their fruitless wait of an hour or two, were observed to be driving off the premises it seemed it was all clear for action.

The cunning teachers had though only driven a short distance away then walked back, where they managed to apprehend several pupils and took their names ready for the big show-down in the morning.

Jim was a bit more cautious than the others and was still approaching, using his best army-cadet-style crawl, when he realised there was a teacher standing only a few feet away from where he was.

He froze.

The teacher failed to spot him in the dark and after a few minutes left.

Phew!!

Knowing that the game was up Jim got back on his bike and cycled home.

The next morning he left early for school, got in without being observed, and carefully applied paper clips to the strings of the upright piano used to accompany the morning's assembly hymn then, again unobserved, made his exit.

The strings were suitably hobbled and, when the pianist started to play, a satisfyingly non-musical racket came forth. The hymn was abandoned and the teacher, having looked inside the piano to see what was wrong, instructed the culprit to own up.

He didn't and maybe sixty-five years on it is a bit late to suspend him now that he has at last confessed.

It was however the only 'jape' performed by the leavers that year and those caught were given a good telling off and sent home in disgrace. I believe the tradition died after that, so Jim's sabotage of the piano brought down the final curtain.

Honestly!

Jim, you are a naughty boy.

CHAPTER SIXTEEN

Breaking The Rules

Jim's first year at Saint Luke's was spent in a large Victorian mansion where he shared a room with Mark. It was so different for students then compared to those in the 2020's; Jim's lodging was full board with three cooked meals a day, a room-cleaner/bedmaker, and a laundry allowance. In those days students were spoilt rotten but of course only a very small percentage of his peers went to college or university. Most went straight into apprenticeships or, for girls in particular, repetitive manual labour in factories until they married and became full-time housewives and mothers.

Jim got on well with his room-mate, who was a very talented conjurer and chess player. He taught Jim the card game Cribbage which they played in any spare moments.

Although students may have been spoilt in some ways, they were kept under close supervision. They had to be in their residences by 8 p.m. every week-day, extended to 10 p.m. on a week-end as long as they first requested permission.

Jim had brought his cycle to Exeter on the train and cycled to Exmouth at least once a week to meet up with Julia. The road was extremely hilly and, as I have told you, Jim's bike gearing was, unknown to him, not designed for such terrain but as I have already commented it no doubt continued to do his muscles a power of good.

Julia also had her cycle at college so on fine days they were able to meet in the country for a bit of a cuddle in privacy. I wonder why they needed that.

On winter days they would meet in a park or along the sea-front, treating themselves to a mug of tea and Welsh Rarebit in a café, this being the cheapest thing on the menu, basically cheese on toast with a fried egg on top. As both of them were on full rations paid for by the college they had no need of anything more substantial.

Jim had only just escaped spending two years training to defend his country. Many students had not been so fortunate, or maybe unfortunate, depending on your point of view. These students had the experience of two years in the army so were not fresh out of school and wet behind the ears. They had experienced the outside world during the 'cold war' and were much more mature than our Jim.

One of them, Roger Pedlar, was in the same lodgings as Jim and took Jim under his wings.

One of his services was to give Jim a 'johnnie'; he felt anyone courting should 'be prepared', though not in the 'Boy Scouts' way I guess.

However it was nearly a year before it was used, on a glorious summer's day on the local common.

One's 'first time' for many men and women is not always a pleasant memory for all sorts of reasons, as the best-selling book and film 'On Chesil Beach', set at around the same time as Jim's first time, makes painfully obvious, but Jim treasures the memory of that day as one of utter bliss.

Hopefully Julia feels the same way.

St Luke's was very much a sportsman's dream but Jim was not into any sports so he found other things to do in his spare moments, of which there were plenty. He started a Gramophone Club, which met weekly to listen to and discuss classical pieces.

Hoping to carry on his acting career he auditioned for a part in a Peter Ustinoff play. The role needed Jim to adopt an American accent, and Jim, similarly to his inability to speak French with other than a strong Dorset accent, proved unable to speak Yankee, so his life on the stage ground to a halt and never recovered, although as I have already said he continued to act off-stage for the rest of his life.

Not being awarded a part he was instead put in charge of the sound and lighting, a role he enjoyed which also led to him being a projectionist when the college showed a hired film.

He loved playing the concert grand piano in the main theatre and kept up his organ lessons, though his skills were well below that expected by his teacher. However he was permitted to play Exeter Cathedral organ on one occasion which he found awesome. He also inveigled his way into the woodwork department and built a small four-heddle loom, several lyres and a radiogram.

The radiogram deserves a paragraph or two of its own.

For some reason, lost in the midst of time, students were not allowed to have a wireless (radio) in their rooms. In fact Jim's room for his first year did not even have a 13-amp socket when Jim first occupied it. This was soon rectified as there was a socket the other side of the partition wall between his room and the hallway outside. Perhaps best not to investigate what happened next. Although it was not illegal in those days as it is now it was certainly against college regulations.

Jim was only following in his father's footsteps as, when the BBC started broadcasting programmes for schools, his dad had run a cable from the roof of the nearby canteen across to his outside classroom and was thus able to treat his classes to the occasional broadcast. Came an inspection and the radio and the electrical connection was noticed. Jim's dad was told he should not have taken things into his own hands and was told to remove the cable. When he protested that, in providing mains power to his classroom, he was only trying to enhance his pupils' education he was told

"But nobody asked you to!"

This became something of a family joke from then on when someone, with the best of intentions, did something that got them into trouble.

These were still the days when valves were considered superior to the new-fangled transistors so Jim sent for a kit for a valve VHF (another new innovation) tuner (the first stage in a radio) which he built at home over the holidays. Clive Sinclair had produced a very small and acoustically excellent amplifier which did use transistors and Jim bought one to go with his tuner.

The radio signals may have been 'wireless' compared to their predecessor, the telegraph; the inside workings of the tuner were certainly not. However with his dad's help they managed to successfully adjust the various coils and eventually, with the aid of a two metre long aerial, picked up the BBC's VHF broadcast.

Now of course the equipment needed installing in a cabinet with the addition of a record player which, as I mentioned above, was then called a gramophone, hence 'radiogram'. On his return to college Jim designed a cabinet and built it in the woodwork room. When finished it was installed in his room.

News of this student breaking the college rules big time reached the college principal who visited to see if the rumour was true.

Jim fully expected to be in severe trouble but much to his surprise the principal instead seemed to admire his initiative and craftsmanship and went away with no further comment.

Jim continued to enjoy his radio and records until the day he left. This was the beginning of 'The Swinging Sixties' and the young of the world were overturning the old regimes left, right, and centre.

Jim did his bit!

CHAPTER SEVENTEEN

Learning To Teach

At the end of Jim's first year at college, Julia completed with distinction her two year course and was appointed to a Junior School in South Somerset, impressing her colleagues and much enriching her pupils with her teaching skills.

Jim hitch-hiked up the A30/A303 about once a month to visit his beloved.

He never had trouble getting a lift there and back, once on a motorbike which terrified him and once thinking he was going to be kidnapped by a lady who seemed desperate for a slave to satisfy her every whim; well that is what he says, but unlike his mother...(see Page Three!).

On one of his trips to visit Julia he went with other students on a minibus to a show in London. On the way back, around midnight, he left the transport to walk the mile or two down the road leading to Julia's village. Once the minibus went out of sight he was alone in the dark.

Dark it certainly was. With an overcast sky and no moon it was the first time he had experienced utter darkness. Nothing was visible, not the hedges, not even his own feet. He has never again known such a profound blackness.

Feeling his way along the hedgerow he eventually came to the outskirts of the village and some blessed light. He made his way to the car park where the local bus company left their double decker bus prior to its early morning departure. He climbed aboard and slept until dawn on the upstairs back seat.

Fortunately he awoke and alighted before the driver and conductor arrived when he would have had some explaining to do or, if they had not noticed him, found himself on an unexpected tour of Somerset.

During the long summer holiday, between the two year course to become a qualified teacher, the students had to come up with an educational tool of some sort.

When Jim was ten years old his teacher taught him how to make plaster casts.

In case you are tempted to try it yourself I should warn you that Plaster of Paris sets at a very high temperature.

A few years back a girl was making a plaster model and had her hands in the wet plaster when it set, which it does quite suddenly. The heat destroyed eight of her fingers as they were trapped inside the hot solid plaster.

Don't believe me? Google 'Plaster of Paris Accident'.

The correct method, which Jim was taught, is to make a clay model from which is made a pair of plaster cast moulds. The final model is made using these and a liberal quantity of Vaseline to stop the final plaster model sticking to the mould.

Young Jim and a friend, having made several small wall decorations in this manner, set out to make a large plaster model of Dorset, using an ordnance survey map to get the correct positions and heights of the features.

This precious item had been stored by Jim's proud dad so Jim made good use of his childhood model to fulfil, in just a short while, the educational tool requested by his college tutor.

Jim wrote the names of rivers, towns, hills, bays and of course Chesil Beach, on card flags attached to cocktail sticks and drilled holes golf-course style in his model in the correct places. The idea was that pupils would be given the blank model and have to decide into which hole each flag should be placed, so learning the geography of, in this case, Dorset.

Jim's dad took him and his model back to Exeter where his tutor was mightily impressed, giving Jim full marks and an excellent rating.

He never admitted that he had actually made the model at the age of ten a full eight years' earlier.

Sometimes silence is indeed golden!

Sadly the model came to a dramatic end a good few years later when Jim's dad was moving it one day and dropped it. Plaster of Paris does not take kindly to being dropped but Jim treasures a photo of his award winning sculpture.

You may be wondering why the college was called 'Teachers' Training' as I may have given you the impression that Jim does everything else except train for his future role. That is some-what true as his Music and Maths courses were centred around developing the students to a higher level, with little of how best to pass on their learning to the future generation.

However each student was allocated a pupil from a local school to visit at their home and help with their education. Jim was allocated a girl whose name he has sadly forgotten. Meeting her and her parents made a nice break for an hour a two a week for a term. I wonder if she still remembers Jim.

The main training consisted of two 'teaching practices' in local schools.

The first of these was in Cullumpton; a class of eleven year olds who Jim realises, looking back, were not as much under the full control of their regular teacher as they could have been.

Jim found it tough going and he thinks he came close to being advised to choose a different occupation.

His lecturer came to observe Jim's teaching and, in front of Jim, made a comment to a girl that 'He knew what she was up to and she was to stop it.' Jim did not have a clue what this was about but the comment stuck in his memory and in later life he realised that the pupil must have been 'making eyes' at him, a risk all teachers have to learn to manage.

Maybe 'Lolita', published in 1955, should have been on the list of required reading for all students.

The second teaching practice a year later was in Ashburton, a small town on the outskirts of Dartmoor.

This time he had a class of nine and ten year olds under the strict but loving care of Miss Luxton. Because she had her pupils under superb control the teaching of them was much easier and Jim suddenly found that maybe he did have the makings of a teacher after all.

His visiting tutors were also pleased at his improvement.

Every student was visited once by an external examiner and it was arranged that he would join Jim during a music lesson. Jim decided to feature the Smetana composition, Vltava, which represents in sound the route of the river Vltava from source to sea. He prepared an illustrated map showing the various things portrayed by the composer and this went very well, so he gained high praise from his inspector.

To this day when Classic FM plays Vltava, as they often do (when they are not playing Scheherazade) he is immediately transported back to that school hall and his lovely country pupils.

Miss Luxton also took to Jim, although he was given a telling off for allowing another music lesson to run over time, thus reducing the time for an arithmetic session.

"When the bell goes one lesson must end and the next one start. No exceptions!"

One more 'lesson' Jim learnt well and he is still a stickler for being on time.

However his mentor must have been pleased with Jim's teaching as when it came time to return to college he was offered a job at the school. He was tempted, though by then his future path was changing and so Ashburton Junior School remains just a fond memory.

◆ ◆ ◆

Before we leave Ashburton for good though, we will pay a brief visit to Jim's lodgings with the school's headmaster.

The head's wife was Cornish and on several evenings she produced enormous Cornish Pasties, each one overlapping the rim of a large dinner plate.

This was Jim's first experience of a Cornish Pastie, though not his last. However he has never tasted a better one.

The stay was also memorable for Jim's first encounter with 'Under Milk Wood'.

There were two other students in the same digs, both teaching at the secondary school. One of them, Welsh to the core, knew Dylan Thomas's radio play off by heart and entertained the others each evening by reciting it in parts in a glorious strong Welsh accent.

Like Vlatava and Cornish Pasties, Jim can never hear, or watch, Under Milk Wood without being transported back to that magical room in deepest Devon.

Thanks largely to Miss Luxton, Jim passed his teaching practice with flying colours and was also getting the hang of the higher mathematics he was studying.

In view of this he was persuaded to stay on at college for an extra year to take a Diploma in Mathematics at Exeter University. Then, as now, secondary mathematics teachers were in short supply.

The extra year went more or less according to plan. Jim gave up music for Technical Drawing, gaining an extra 'A' level.

He gained his diploma and so was set up for a career in a secondary school although this could well have not been his future path as part of the extra year was teaching in a secondary modern, the one pupils went to if they 'failed' the eleven plus.

He was assigned to a school in Plymouth and the first day there he was terrified by the older pupils, the like of whom he had never before come across.

As with his jellyfish sting sparing him from a cadet camp, his skin literally saved him for a second time, though this time it probably altered the whole course of the rest of his life.

On his second day at the school Jim developed a severe rash and the college matron panicked. It was at this same time that Cardiff had a severe outbreak of smallpox which killed nineteen people before it was brought under control by mass vaccinations.

Many of Jim's fellow students were Welsh and the Matron decided that she could not take the risk that Jim had contracted smallpox and sent him home to his parents.

Jim therefore had no experience of teaching older pupils until he was in his first job. He is pretty sure that he would have so struggled to control his classes in the Plymouth Secondary Modern that he would have never countenanced teaching such an age range and switched back to Juniors.

Thankfully he did not have smallpox, just an extra holiday, and probably a bad attack of acne.

For the rest of the year he attended Exeter Hospital for ultraviolet light treatment which his mates found hilarious as it gave Jim apparent severe sunburn in the depths of winter. It may have amused them but it little affected the rash. He still suffers.

CHAPTER EIGHTEEN

Mr & Mrs

Jim applied for a job in Box Hill, Surrey.

He seemed to be the only candidate and was warmly welcomed. However he was told at his interview that he was expected to supervise inter-school rugby matches each Saturday. This was way out of Jim's comfort zone. He told the headmaster that of rugby he knew very little and cared about even less. They must have been desperate as he was still offered the job.

He asked for a few hours to decide if he would accept and looked at accommodation and house prices in the area. This was in the commuter belt for London and very upmarket. Although set in beautiful countryside with magnificent houses it rapidly became obvious that he would be in severe financial difficulties making ends meet there.

With that plus the unwelcome supervision of rugby matches, he turned the job down. Jim has never regretted doing this and feels it was very much a wise decision.

He then applied for a post in a Secondary Modern in Balsall Heath, part of Birmingham, and also for one in a Northants Grammar School. He was offered an interview at both within days of applying.

Having looked at the situation of Balsall Heath he decided that a Grammar School in the country was a much better option, so he caught the train to, what was then if not now, a delightfully quiet English rural town. I think the headmaster would have given Jim the job sight unseen as it was the shortest interview imaginable.

Basically:

"Can you tell me your name?"

"Yes. Jim Wright"

"That's right Mr Wright. You've got the job."

So Jim started his career in a boys' Grammar School.

He was never asked to supervise rugby matches although he was regularly roped into adding up each term's marks for one of the physical training teachers.

We have come a little too far down the road.

I expect that you are wondering about Julia.

Never fear, the relationship had continued to blossom and on Julia's twenty-first birthday they were engaged. They hitch-hiked to Taunton to buy the ring.

There being plenty of jewellers much nearer to her home, Jim cannot remember why they chose Taunton. He thinks Julia must have seen the ring she fancied in a Taunton shop as there was a regular bus service to the town from her South Somerset village where, you may remember, she had been teaching for the past year.

Portlanders are an independent race and not so keen on foreigners from across the causeway, calling them 'kimberlins', so Julia marrying one of them was another possible snag.

However this problem eased when Jim informed Julia's parents that his mum was born a Portlander, her parents having lived on the Portland estate at which her dad was head gardener. Later this seal of approval was reinforced when Jim found out that one of his great-great-grandfathers on his mother's side was a Portland stone-mason.

I think both sets of parents must have been all too well aware of how young their offspring were to be getting married.

Although a nearly twenty-two year old bride was nothing unusual, the groom would often be quite a few years older than his intended and probably would have had several failed romances behind him. This was certainly not the case for Jim, whose previous romances totalled to zero.

However if Jim and Julia wanted to set up home together they would have to be married. Living together unmarried was far from the normal behaviour it has now become and would certainly have horrified both Jim's and Julia's parents.

It seems certain, nevertheless, that our Jim had no doubts as to his desire to marry Julia.

Maybe Julia was not quite so sure that she was doing the right thing but she was swept up in the avalanche that was Jim at full speed downhill.

Once marriage plans start to be made, wedding gift lists issued, guests invited, church and reception booked and so on, it is hard indeed for any bride or groom to fail to say 'I do'.

So in early August, Jim having just turned twenty-one, Jim and Julia became Mr and Mrs and set off by train on their two night honeymoon to Stratford-upon-Avon.

Jim nearly spent his first night as a married man on his own.

When their train reached Bristol he left it to buy some drinks from the platform buffet. He had only just climbed back into the carriage when the train pulled out.

Another few seconds and the bride would, on her wedding day,

have been left to her fate like Miss Havisham in Great Expect-
ations, although unlike her she would at least have been married
before being abandoned.

With them being short of funds the chosen guest house for their
two-night honeymoon stay was far from a palace; more a grotty
terrace.

When they were shown to their room it was replete with two
single beds, far apart and seemingly fixed firmly to the floor.

It was either spend their honeymoon night in separate beds or
try to get some sleep together in a narrow single one.

"Well, here's another nice mess you've gotten me into." Julia
might well have complained to Jim, echoing Hardy's catch
phrase to Laurel when things went wrong, as it did in all of the
silent movies Jim used to show.

 What a mistake Jim had made indeed.

Yet another one.

Are you still counting?

They decided on Option Two but it was far from comfortable
and perhaps Jim should not have been as surprised as he was
when he woke to find himself alone in bed, alone in the room,
and, as he soon discovered, alone in the guest-house.

Where was his lovely bride?

Jim panicked.

Was his wife of less than twenty-four hours to be found at the
bottom of the Avon which flowed through Shakespeare's home
town?

Had she been abducted by a jealous ex-boyfriend?

Had she run home to mother? Their suitcases were still in the room so it seemed unlikely.

Shades of his father all those years ago coming home to be told by his landlady that his wife had left, though they had at least managed to last more than one night of married bliss.

Jim panicked.

Yes, I know I have said that already.

Panic does that to people.

He decided that he had better let the police know that his wife was missing, presumed drowned.

At the Police Station a very patient police sergeant took down the description of Jim's missing partner. He was watched by a fellow constable.

When it came to describing the events leading up to the disappearance, the look on both policemen's faces said it all.

I mentioned the novel 'On Chesil Beach' a few pages back. It was written many years after Jim and Julia's honeymoon and not by me, sadly, though the situation painted in it bears an uncanny resemblance to Jim and Julia's; although as you know, our two were hardly the 'first-timers' the couple are in that book.

To their eternal credit the policemen managed to avoid collapsing into peals of laughter and told Jim to go search the town and riverbank to see if he could find his bride and come back in the evening if he could not find her.

He did just that.

Relief!

There she was, walking back along the bank of the Avon and seemingly not in great distress or threatening to 'plunge into the billowy wave' like Tit Willow did in The Mikado.

Jim was overjoyed.

He let the police know that he had found his wife and decided it was best not to enquire further as to why Julia had gone for a long early morning walk.

They did the sights, had lunch, went to the theatre and never discussed the matter again.

Maybe it was a bad start but at least they were still together.

The second night though they used both single beds.

Their sleeping arrangements did not get much better when they arrived in their new town, although they did at least have a double bed.

Jim's headmaster had not found it easy to arrange accommodation for them. Eventually he had found a lady in a nearby village with a room to spare who would take Jim and Julia in as paying guests.

She was recently widowed and still grieving for her husband. Although she had offered accommodation out of the goodness of her heart found it very hard to tolerate the reality of two young marrieds who were enjoying so much what they were now officially entitled to do: 'With my body I thee worship'.

It became clear that the situation was not going to work for very long, although their landlady did appreciate Jim using his DIY skills to sort out some faults with the house.

Julia had landed a job teaching in a Junior School in the town and, a few weeks after she started there, one of her colleagues told her that the flat opposite the school was available for rent, which was welcome news.

Jim and Julia moved there, staying for the next four years whilst they saved up enough to pay the deposit for a mortgage.

CHAPTER NINETEEN

Not Having An Enema

Only a couple of months into their marriage Jim wondered for the second time if it was going to be a very short one as along came the Cuban Missile Crisis.

I guess most of us living in the 2020's do not give too much thought to the number of nuclear missiles still ready to fire in retaliation for an attack. Climate change seems a much bigger threat than the mutually assured destruction of a nuclear war.

Back in the 1950's/1960's this seemed all too real a threat to the future of mankind.

When President Kennedy was told that the USSR was installing nuclear missiles just down the road in Cuba, the world did come very close to annihilation.

Each morning for a fortnight Jim and Julia said their goodbyes as they left for their schools, both wondering if they would meet again this side of the grave.

If indeed there was enough of them left to need a grave.

Or come to that anyone left to dig it.

Local councils produced pamphlets giving guidance on how to remove the house doors and use them to make a nuclear shelter, having first piled bags of garden soil onto them. These guides also gave helpful (?) advice on making a temporary toilet and what to do with dead relatives.

Did anyone ever do a dry run of this advice?

Jim and Julia certainly did not remove any doors and their tiny garden would not have yielded the soil to fill many sacks.

They were all too well aware of how little good it would do.

Even if it worked and they survived, what would be left of the world when, after the recommended three days, they rose again?

On Sunday 28th October 1962, after several days of high tension and, entirely due to Kennedy standing alone in refusing the advice of all his military to bomb the sites in Cuba, the situation was defused. The popular US president reasoned that Khrushchev, his opposite number in the USSR, would be no keener on destroying the planet than he was.

Jim and Julia did not much fancy that either.

Kennedy who, if ever anyone deserves to be thanked for the world still being habitable all these years later, proved to be right in his belief.

Khrushchev, much to the world's relief, agreed terms to remove the missiles from Cuba if the USA removed theirs from Turkey and promised not to attack the island.

The crisis was over but, by all the detailed accounts released since then, it was indeed a very close run thing.

That Kennedy was so cruelly and pointlessly assassinated barely a year after he had single-handedly saved the world from mutual destruction was a dreadful thing.

We can only speculate about what he might have achieved in the years ahead. What is certain is that his death shocked the whole world.

Sadly though he was not the first American President to be murdered. The tally stands at four, though several more have had lucky escapes.

Let's hope that total never increases, although Jim might have been sorely tempted if he had found himself armed and in the proximity of at least one recent one.

Jim's first year of teaching was a very steep learning curve, particularly where discipline was concerned.

Julia, now in her third year of teaching, was very understanding and gave Jim much helpful advice.

One problem was that he was only older than his oldest pupils by a matter of three years so he lacked the authority of age whilst the respect of pupils had to be earnt.

His most traumatic experience was soon after he arrived when it was his turn to supervise the whole school as they assembled in the hall each morning.

The more experienced staff could silence pupils just by being there but that morning, alone on the stage, Jim was ignored.

Losing his cool at his inability to shut them up, he demanded they all returned at mid-morning break. This, no doubt anticipating more 'fun', they did.

Jim was still unable to get them quiet. To his credit he stood his ground for fifteen minutes until the bell went for lessons to commence.

Jim by then was a nervous wreck and went to his headmaster ready to give teaching up and switch to gardening or anything that did not require the obedience of teenagers.

Seeing that Jim had reached a crisis point his headmaster, quite correctly, told him that he would gain the respect of his pupils in time and sent him back to his class.

The headmaster did speak to the school prefects who could have, and perhaps should have, supported Jim in his efforts at crowd control. The next day he received an apology from the headboy and a set of small red wine glasses which he still has in his possession.

Things improved from then on, although Jim throughout his career thought that his discipline was not as good as it needed to be.

Much to his surprise one ex-pupil meeting him as an adult many years later commented how strict he had been!

It was good that many ex-pupils took the trouble to speak to him but he was made all too aware of the passing years when another one came up to Jim long after he had retired with the comment

"You're Mr Wright aren't you? Gosh! I didn't expect you to still be around!"

During the time that Jim and Julia lived in the Midlands there was an increasing number of immigrants, many of Indian and Pakistani extraction.

Because of the ready availability of cheaper Victorian terrace housing many immigrant families came to the Midlands' towns and pooled resources to be able to buy or rent a property. This meant that there were often far more occupants of a single house than the number for which it was originally designed.

Almost like a tidal wave roaring up the street, the original white householders sold up and moved out. Soon whole areas of the old town became mainly immigrant.

This affected Julia in her teaching at her junior school as more and more of the pupils were first generation immigrants. For most pupils English was not their first language, although they picked it up much more easily than their parents. Talking to mum and dad about their children was difficult.

Jim and Julia's ground-floor flat was the property of a white couple who also owned a farm in Rhodesia.

In 1965 the 95% white government of Rhodesia, which since 1923 had been self-governing although still part of the British

Empire, declared itself an independent sovereign state.

The minority white rulers, led by Ian Smith, knew that the proposal for them to become part of the British Commonwealth would have meant the introduction of a democratic one person one vote election that was certain to bring in a black government and the consequential loss of their comfortable colonial life-style.

Although internationally condemned, this situation continued with much internal violence until 1980, when the country became part of the British Commonwealth under the African name of Zimbabwe with Robert Mugabe as ruler and that's another sorry story.

Jim's landlords saw the trouble brewing, sold up their Rhodesian property, and moved back to the UK. They used the upstairs of their house while Jim and Julia continued to rent the bottom half plus the cellar where Jim continued his woodworking.

Our young couple was somewhat shocked when their landlords suggested that they had a session giving each other enemas!

Needless to say, I hope, the suggestion was not acted upon and Jim is happy to assure you that an enema, let alone 'a four-some', is an experience not (yet) suffered (or enjoyed?) in his eighty plus years on this earth.

The same goes for a 'three-some'!

Holiday times were mainly spent at home or at their parents as they were saving up to put down the deposit on a house but, having had a somewhat disastrous honeymoon, they decided to splash out for the next summer holiday with a trip by train and boat to Unst, the most northerly inhabited Shetland island.

That there was oil and gas in abundance under the North Sea had not yet been discovered and Unst was just a small farming community, although the week they were there it coincided with the annual Shetland farmers' get-together, so it was quite lively.

Not only the farmers were lively, the Shetland ponies were too. They gave Jim and Julia a fright when, as they walked across the open country, a herd started chasing them at stampede speed. These stocky animals could well have caused them considerable harm but Jim and Julia managed, adrenaline fuelled, to outrun them.

It was as well that they were not injured as there was only the most basic of medical treatment available on Unst, the nearest hospital being a boat ride south to the capital of Lerwick in the main island.

Before they left Jim was offered the vacant teaching job at Unst village school.

He was not encouraged to seriously consider this when told that the vacancy had arisen due to the death, during the last winter, of the previous incumbent after she suffered an inflamed appendix.

The sea was too rough to ship her to the hospital and her appendix ruptured and killed her.

Being told this sad story did little to incite Jim and Julia to consider moving to Unst no matter how beautiful it was on a summer's day with over eighteen hours of daylight in June, yet under six hours in December.

CHAPTER TWENTY

Scooter On The Loose

During the years spent in the flat Jim progressed from a bicycle to a scooter, made by the French company Motobécane, to a Bond three-wheeler minicar.

The transition from a bicycle to a scooter was easy for Jim and he soon applied for a driving test.

On turning up at the test centre he was given a route to follow and sent off to follow it. On his return he was told that he had passed. Jim has no idea what evidence there was that he was safe to be on the road. He presumes that, as he returned within the time allowed for the route, without a police escort, and intact, then he must be OK to take off his L-plates.

Julia decided that she too would learn to ride the scooter and she took to the road, Jim having first explained the working of the gears and clutch.

She had not gone more than a few feet when she panicked and leapt off the machine which, having a low centre of gravity, carried on at a sedate pace in first gear without her on board.

Jim raced after it, lifted the rear driving wheel off the ground to stop it going any further, then managed to reach the key and switch off the engine.

This experience so traumatised Julia that she never tried again, though she enjoyed (Jim thinks) many miles as a pillion passenger.

Jim only kept the scooter for a year. English winters then, if not so much it seems now in these days of the climate crisis, were not conducive to such a mode of transport.

He discovered that his motorcycle driving licence was valid for driving a three-wheeler car; this remained true until 2001. It seems another strange decision by those set above us, joining the decision to permit Jim's mum to drive alone during Suez without passing a test.

However, as a motor-bike and sidecar have three wheels, as do motorised tricycles, it may have seemed simpler to define all three-wheeled vehicles as motor-cycles even when they were obviously no such thing if they had a steering wheel and the three pedals of a (non-automatic) car.

Perhaps it is stranger still that nowadays a four-wheel car driving licence does not permit one to drive a two wheeler, though it does qualify you to drive a three-wheeler but not a motorbike and sidecar.

Do you want a moment to read that again?! The whole area is a mass of conundrums. Have fun with Dr Google!

Whatever, in 1967 what Jim was planning to do was perfectly legal, so he set off to Northampton to exchange his scooter for a Bond Minicar. Surviving specimens of this aluminium-based vehicle, the first models of which were produced in 1949, are now classics and like hens' teeth with only twenty-five taxed in the UK in 2020. Even if you could find a seller, it would have a price to reflect its rarity.

There were not many around even in the 1960's. The whole production run was under 25 000 vehicles in seventeen years. Reliant Robins far outsold them, in spite of the Bond being more stable on sharp corners. Production of the Bond Minicar in its many versions ceased in 1966. Again if you are interested in such things there are several informative articles on the net.

Let's get back to 1966 where Jim has just bought his first (three-wheeler) car. The Northampton garage owner took Jim for a short demonstration run, explained what the three pedals were for, and left Jim to learn to drive on his own!

The car was powered, though that is arguably putting it too strongly, by a Villiers197cc two-stroke motorbike engine which was bolted to the upright central front wheel, driving said wheel with a short chain.

Let's not dwell too long on that first drive back home.

Suffice to say that a lamp-post had a lucky escape but after the first twenty miles Jim just about got the hang of it although he was soaked with sweat by the time he re-joined Julia.

Because it used a motorcycle engine the car did not have reverse gears. To compensate for this the steering turned the front wheel ninety-degrees each way so the car would turn in its own length.

This was demonstrated to the horror of his watching colleagues when he first took his new pride and joy to school.

Not having fully mastered clutch control and having turned the front wheel to ninety degrees to avoid the car parked in front of his, Jim failed to turn it back to zero fast enough and, mounting the grass island at the front of the school, did a full 360 degree turn before exiting.

Mostly though the ability to 'turn on a sixpence' did make a reverse gear unnecessary.

Top speed (going forwards) was about 50 mph downhill. Going uphill this reduced to that of a plodding heavily laden mule.

The vehicle was ridiculously noisy and under-powered but Jim and Julia loved it and drove many hundreds of miles in it over the next few years complete with babies in baskets behind them; there were no rear seats, just an empty space.

Eventually Jim borrowed his dad's car (four wheels) and passed his car driving test, so was able to sell on the three-wheeler and move on to more traditional transport.

After four years living in the flat Jim and Julia had saved enough for the deposit on a semi-detached house on the outskirts of the town, priced at £3100, and in case you misunderstand, that was the price of the house, not the deposit.

Mind you, a new teacher was only earning around £1000 a year.

One problem in their new abode soon made itself evident when it came to his no-reverse-gear car.

I guess Jim could have parked it on the road outside, as he had at the flat, but in those days house garages, if indeed they had one, which Jim's did, were generally used to house a vehicle rather than being, as now, regarded as a convenient storage space for anything not actually wanted in the main house.

Furthermore, cars parked on the road had to display a light of some sort at night. Jim had a paraffin-fuelled hurricane lamp which did the trick but this was a fag, so moving the car onto his property was a better option, once he could work out how to do it.

The answer, as Isaac Newton discovered, was gravity. Let's not get involved in what exactly that is. Let's just be glad it exists.

The house was on a hill so, by driving up the road past his gate-way for about twenty–five yards and putting the car into neutral, it was possible to build up enough speed and momentum going backwards to take the car up and over the pavement and through the entrance onto the drive, which then sloped gently down to the garage.

That Jim managed this for several years without any mishap to his car, his gate-posts, or a hapless passer-by, either pays credit to his great skill as a driver or more likely to the concerned care of St Christopher.

◆ ◆ ◆

In those far off times a couple who had been married for more than a year or two with no children to show for it were perceived to be lacking in the knowledge of, or possibly the desire to undertake, the procedure necessary to start a baby.

Jim had been taking precautions for the first few years, assuming that, once he stopped this, a baby would be along nine months later. That turned out not to be a divine right and, after a few months 'living dangerously', concerns began to creep in, although Jim is pretty certain that he and Julia were indeed 'doing it right'.

Various methods were adopted and temperatures were taken (Julia's that is) and the recommended right foods were eaten, or avoided.

All to no avail.

Eventually they decided that they must be barren and, lacking the intervention of a helpful heavenly being as God provided for Abraham's wife, would have to adopt a baby instead.

They were duly interviewed and told that they would qualify to raise someone else's child.

This action did the trick with whoever keeps an eye on such matters as the next month Julia missed her period. Two months later the doctor confirmed that a baby was on its way.

We are way before the days of pregnancy tests and scans, so it was just a case of wait and see. The baby was due in mid-December. Not a good time to have a birthday in Jim's opinion (although his mother's mum, Gran, was born on Christmas Day) but as I said, although deeply desired, the advent of the newcomer was rather unplanned.

CHAPTER TWENTY-ONE

Making Friends With An Enemy

Another unplanned event was due to Jim going into the local electrical retailer during the summer to buy a light bulb. The firm was running a competition. It was officially for anyone who bought a radio but they gave Jim an entry form anyway.

The competition involved designing a Yale key to fit the exposed tumblers of a lock and the prize was a long weekend for two in Rudesheim in the Rhine Valley during the Octoberfest which celebrates (and how!) the successful harvest of that year's grapes.

The entrant also had to give a reason why they wanted to win this holiday and Jim wrote '..because I love to go a wandering'.

In September came a letter telling him, much to his surprise, that he had won.

Julia, being over seven months pregnant by the late October date of the holiday, did not want to risk travelling, so her brother, John, came in her place.

Such holidays were far from commonplace in the early 1960's. When Jim and John reached the Midlands airport the departure lounge was a large marquee whilst the DC4 plane was a converted war-time one. It shook and shuddered and made conversation nigh-on impossible but, unlike Jim's first flight as a cadet, at least he could see out of the window.

Perhaps it would have been better if he had not been able to for, during the flight, one of the engines caught fire and had to be shut down. The other three were OK which is as well as otherwise Jim's story would end here. They landed in the depths of the Black Forest and, through a raging storm, were transferred by coach to their hotel in Rudesheim.

Unlike most of those celebrating the harvest in the many local bars, Jim did not drink alcohol. He found the unfermented grape juice was a good, if less incapacitating, alternative.

Booked onto the same holiday was a party of wives minus husbands from Newcastle and they were great fun.

Jim found himself very much attracted to one of them. The attraction was mutual but apart from a ride together in a two-person cable car nothing that should not have happened did, though they kept up a correspondence for a while on their return, which is not something Jim is very comfortable with.

The first evening in the bar/dance hall Jim and John, his brother-in-law, sat at the same table as a German family. The father had spent some years in captivity in England so spoke English quite well. His daughter, Judith, who was in her early-twenties like John, was not so fluent.

It is a very romantic town and the wine amplifies the effect so it is no surprise that John and Judith took to each other and met up again the following two evenings. Their friendship continued after John returned to England and he later visited Judith at her home and tried to master the German tongue. Although they did consider marriage the barriers seemed too high. Instead they both married folk from their own countries, although they kept in touch throughout John's life until, tragically and much lamented, he died from a brain tumour at the age of seventy.

Although all four engines kept operating throughout the last evening flight home it was still a flight to remember as the plane, for some while though it felt like for ever, flew through a ferocious thunderstorm. The thunder claps and the lightning were terrifying and the plane shook and rattled even more than it had on the way out. More than a few prayers were sent upwards and someone was listening as they safely reached their destination airfield and their homes.

Such was the novelty in the 1960's of Jim's package holiday that he told his class about the adventure (omitting any mention of the hen-party wives).

One of his pupil's parents was the manager of a local arts centre which led to him being asked to speak about his trip to a group on an activity weekend. This he did, illustrating his talk with the 'oom-pa-pa' beer-cellar songs on an LP record which he had bought in Germany and still has. The talk was entitled 'Adventure Through a Light-bulb' which made those attending wonder to what sort of boring scientific exploration they were to be treated and who were no doubt relieved when they found that it was no such thing. Jim thinks the songs went down much better than his talk did.

Can you imagine such an invitation nowadays, or at least pre-Covid?

"So you had a long-weekend in Germany?"

"Big deal!'

Towards the end of November, with Julia's pregnancy nearly to time, Julia gave Jim a scare.

The town had an underground public convenience which Jim and Julia had never needed to make use of. That day, while they were out shopping, Julia was taken short. Jim waited at the top of the steps down and waited, and waited, and then some.

By this time he was visualising Julia giving birth in a cubicle. He asked a lady to go and see if she could find his wife.

She was not there.

More panic.

Eventually Julia appeared. It turned out that the convenience had two entrances quite a way apart and she had exited through the one that she had not entered by. Not realising what she had done, and not being able to see Jim waiting where she thought that she had left him, she assumed that he had impulsively gone to look in some shops and had set off to look for him.

Jim, you do worry a lot don't you? However have you managed to keep most of your hair?

December came, as did the baby due day, but the signs of Julia's body getting ready for the big event were sorely missing. The baby was certainly alive and kicking but Julia's womb was not co-operating. Christmas drew ever closer.

Yet again panic set in.

A ride in the car up a bumpy road did not work, nor did cod-liver oil, nor jumping up and down on the bottom two stairs.

Eventually Julia was admitted to hospital for an induction which did work. After some hours and late at night Jim was kicked out of the hospital as there was no way a father should observe either where babies came from or the end product of his efforts, at least not until it had been washed and dressed.

He arrived home to find their Siamese cat had staged a protest rally by emptying a packet of sugar and spreading it all over the kitchen floor.

The next day Jim managed to dye their undies a nice shade of pink.

The sooner Julia came back home the better!

Julia did not give birth easily and felt that she was treated very harshly by cold-hearted nurses who told her to shut up shouting as she was only doing what every other pregnant creature had done since mammals arrived on the Earth. Suffice to say that the damage, both physically and emotionally, took a long time to get over.

At last, two days before Christmas, Jim and Julia became the proud parents of a baby girl, named Joy.

Much joy she certainly brought them. Tragically she also brought much sadness.

Joy was only a few months old when Julia realised that she was again pregnant and the following February a second girl was born. They named her Helen Elizabeth.

It will not surprise you that Julia refused to go to hospital to give birth to her second child and, thanks to a kind midwife, Jim was able to be in their bedroom to observe that wonderful moment when a new life leaves the comfort of the womb to start its journey in the great outside.

Sadly though, all was not well with Joy.

Julia found red in her wee one May morning and rushed her little girl to the doctor who suggested that Julia had been feeding beetroot to her daughter. Although Julia was adamant that she had done no such thing she was sent home with the instruction to return if there were any more signs of red in her wee.

Julia, far from satisfied with this diagnosis, checked her one-year old daughter over and found a lump in her tummy.

A frantic call to the surgery brought to the house a locum doctor, older and wiser than their usual one, who soon had an ambulance on its way. Julia and Joy returned to the hospital where she had been born. There they confirmed that Joy had a tumour on the kidney.

It is called a Wilm's tumour after the German doctor who first identified it in the 1880's. To be fair to the GP who failed to make a correct diagnosis, it is extremely rare. There are only around 200 cases a year in the UK and then usually in children between three and four years old. The doctor would almost certainly not have come across the cancer in his previous brief career and probably never would again.

Julia was able to stay in the hospital with Joy who was operated on the next day but the surgeon was not able to give a hopeful prognosis as the tumour had spread to other organs.

Over the next months Joy was treated with radiotherapy which, on its own, was terrible for Jim and Julia to observe as at only a year and a half she was too young to understand what was going on.

They tried to make her life as normal as possible, although they feared it was going to be a short one, but they did not give up hope until sometime in October when Julia found another lump in Joy's tummy.

Although it was a hard decision, both Joy's parents and the surgeon agreed that further treatment was only going to cause the little girl more distress and it was decided to let nature take its course.

Julia was so brave through all this terrible time, reading stories to Joy and telling her about Jesus and how beautiful heaven was.

Joy gradually grew thinner and weaker.

One morning an angel came to her in the form of a small black cat which arrived at their back door, made itself at home, cuddled up to Joy and stayed with her until the day she died in her cot a week later, watched over by her parents.

Jim always finds this cat angel hard to believe but he has the last photo he took of Joy and there is the cat sitting close to her so it is not a figment of his imagination. The next day the angel cat left and was never seen again, except perhaps by some other dying child in need of comfort.

If you are counting, this is the second time Jim was in the presence of death. Two to go though none as tragic for him as this one.

Some years later Jim discovered that a granddaughter of Earl Mountbatten had died in 1991 aged five from the same cancer. On learning this sad fact Jim sat on a bench in the Mountbatten's estate, Broadlands, in Hampshire, and sobbed uncontrollably for a long time, heartbroken at the memory it had stirred.

The Mountbattens set up The Leonora Cancer Fund, a trust in their child's name to support parents and help find treatments. It has now merged with another to become The Edwina Mountbatten and Leonora Children's Foundation.

The Wilm's tumour survival rates have improved dramatically over the years but with this tumour being so rare it is hard to give an accurate prediction of the chance of any child diagnosed with it making it to adulthood

. The teachers at Jim's school, and the friends and neighbours of Julia and Jim, were very supportive throughout this sad time but there was no organised support group or counselling in those days, so Jim and Julia had to find their own paths to peace in their hearts.

Julia was helped by having Helen Elizabeth who was only nine months old when Joy died, so was still very dependent on her mother being strong.

Jim thought that having another child would also help them and he was right.

He and Julia must have got the hang of starting babies as it was only a couple of months to Julia finding she was again pregnant.

CHAPTER TWENTY-TWO

Thank You Alexander

By October the new addition to Jim's family was due, though the midwife who had been summoned thought Jim was being premature in calling her in and left the house to do her rounds.

Before she returned though Julia became certain the baby was on its way out and Jim decided he had better get the gas and air working. Having watched the birth of Helen Elizabeth he thought he knew what to do.

Perhaps fortunately for both mother and baby the midwife returned just in time and Jim's son made a speedy journey into the light without needing the keen amateur assistance of his father or, truth to tell, that of the midwife either; her role ended up as being a goalie saving the new born from shooting off the bed onto the floor.

Jim & Julia were delighted to have a son and he grew up to bring much pride to his parents through his achievements as a cameraman, incidentally meeting and filming with many well-known people, including Nelson Mandela, David Attenborough, Geoff Hamilton, Alan Titchmarsh, and Dudley's own Lenny Henry. Jim did, many years later, get to meet Geoff Hamilton's widow as well as Alan and Lenny and they all were fulsome in their praise of his and Julia's gifted son. Equally talented were his son's two daughters who inherited his artistic ability

Also a source of pride was Helen Elizabeth who excelled at everything she turned her hand to. She became a skilled linguist.

So fluent was she in German as a student that the mayor of a German town where she spent a term as part of her higher qualifications mistook her for a local. When he found that she was an English student, he praised her to the skies to her college which led to a feature about her linguistic talents in the local press.

More purring from proud parents.

After a brief time working for a London investment firm Helen switched to being a personal assistant to the owner of a business which sold items mainly from the Far East and the Third World, both as a retailer and a wholesaler.

Sent to organise a stall at a trade fair in Barcelona, she attracted such a lot of orders that she was sent to live in Spain in order to set up a branch of the business there. This proved very successful and to boot she added Catalan to her list of languages.

Although she made several Spanish friends, she missed her family and her home country so after seven years decided to return where, thanks to the internet, she was able for some time to manage the Spanish business from England, commuting to Spain when necessary.

A while later it was sold on, enriching the owner, but sadly not Jim's daughter, by well over a million pounds.

However Lady Luck, or possibly Cupid, smiled on her as her personal life was itself enriched by her meeting a kind and caring man who became her marriage partner and together they raised two talented children.

Once their youngsters were in higher education she became for several years a key member of a team that organized high power conferences for the leaders of various professions such as the police, the government, and the armed forces. As I write this she has now followed in the scholastic family tradition as a support worker for older teenagers at a local school, where she has been called a 'terrific addition to the department'.

◆ ◆ ◆

Jim, like his son and daughter, also met several well-known people during his time teaching in the boys' grammar school.

David Frost was an ex-pupil. He had left the term before Jim started there but Jim met him when he returned a few years later as a successful TV presenter to judge the annual drama competition.

The other well-known folk Jim met were as a result of a cunning ruse by his headmaster who appealed to the great and the good, well the famous anyway, to come to Prize Giving Day, to be rewarded for their kindness by having various rooms named after them. It probably helped that a prestigious Public School bore the same name as his did (apart from the word Grammar) and the two schools, though poles apart in their intake not to mention expense, were often confused.

Possibly, or even probably, the distinguished guests may well have made the same error when they accepted the invitation, not that Jim's school was in any way inferior to the Public one. It gave those fortunate pupils who had passed the eleven plus an excellent all-round education.

When Jim arrived at the school it already had the Fleming, Penny and Cockcroft Science Rooms. While Jim was teaching there, added to the list were The Compton Mackenzie (Library) and The Peter Scott (Biology Room). Also coming to Prize Giving were Douglas Bader, the one-leg-missing pilot made famous in Reach for the Sky, and Lord Boothby, the MP; Jim cannot remember to which rooms they had their names attached but he does remember that Lord Boothby was attached to a rather attractive young female.

Top of Jim's list, to name the new Mountbatten Sports Hall, came the aforementioned Earl Mountbatten, to whom Jim served tea! Jim does not know if this successful idea continued after he left but the school was not to survive as a Grammar School for much longer anyway.

Although hard to believe (but photographic evidence exists!) the new Mountbatten Hall was constructed with Jim's prefab-hut classroom inside it. As the walls of the new hall went up, Jim's classroom became darker and darker and ever noisier as the builders worked on the scaffolding outside. At last, fortunately before the roof of the new hall went on, a portacabin was erected on the school field and Jim was able to move his classes into it.

One week at around this time Jim came close to suffering the same fate as his grandfather who, as you may recall, died from cellulitis after cutting his leg in the garden.

Jim had developed a ganglion on his wrist. This is a cyst on a tendon which caused Jim some pain when playing the piano or the organ so he was given an appointment at a hospital to have the cyst drained. The procedure did not go as it should have since the doctor snapped the needle of the syringe he was using. When he asked the nurse for a replacement she said she had none but she would go to get one and left the room. The doctor however found one and proceeded to drain the cyst.

Jim well remembers the shocked look on the nurse's face when she returned with a sterile needle, only to be told it was all right as the doctor had found a spare.

This would be the end of that story, and pretty boring, if it had not been for the fact that the next morning Jim awoke to find his arm swollen like one of those frogs who can blow themselves up to frighten off a predator. He rushed to his GP who was very concerned and diagnosed cellulitis. This was treated with a course of a very powerful antibiotic which saved Jim from the same end as his grandfather. Jim blames the hospital doctor for using a second-hand needle. We will never know if that is right, though it seems highly likely.

◆ ◆ ◆

We should not leave our Midland town without a mention of Jim's church-going. Soon after he moved to the town he joined a group of church organists, becoming their treasurer. He was often asked to play for services at different churches in the town. He also regularly played for the services at the local borstal, a prison for youths, which was an interesting experience and we hope the only time Jim will find himself in jail, although I guess he is a bit too old (and some) for a borstal incarceration.

Another time a chapel organist went sick just as rehearsals for a performance of an oratorio had started. Jim did his best to learn the not so easy music and rehearsed the choir. He fully expected to play for the scheduled live performance. He was therefore more than a little disappointed when, on the appointed day, the sick organist had a miraculous recovery and sent Jim packing so that she could take the honours.

Mendelsohn may have been relieved as Jim is not that good an organist but it left a nasty taste as they say.

With the immigrant population growing at a huge rate a new estate was developed in what had been green fields when Jim bought his house. Included in this was a hall cum church which was an innovative concept at the time. During secular activities the small chancel section was screened off with sliding doors. Jim heard that the new church was looking for someone to organise a choir and put his name forward. He doubts there were many others after the job but he got it anyway and he much enjoyed several years in the role.

Jim has particularly fond memories of a Nativity Play because of one young lad who sang the last verse of 'In the Bleak Midwinter'; you know 'What can I bring him, Poor as I am...'

This lad had been referred to Jim by his mother as she was concerned that her son was 'tone deaf'. Jim took up the challenge and, finding that the boy could distinguish a high note from a lower one, gave him several singing lessons; he was soon singing like a canary.

During the last verse of the carol at the end of the nativity play the same lad, now a shepherd-boy, had everyone present in tears with the beauty of his voice.

The Bishop of the region at that time was very much of the High-Church Anglo-Catholic tradition, whilst the priest appointed to Jim's church, Paul, was leaning much more towards the simplicity of the non-conformists, as did Jim. Paul became a close friend but all too soon he was appointed to a new parish and the church was left to fend for itself. I guess you will not be too surprised to learn that Jim, as choir-master, took it upon himself to look after the well-being of the church and its parishioners.

After many months a new priest was appointed. Unlike his predecessor he was one who followed the Anglo-Catholic tradition of his bishop. He brought to the humble church hall large candles, incense, and a statue of the Virgin Mary.

For many of his parishioners this was not what they had become used to or it seems what they wanted. They raised their concerns with Jim. He tried to persuade them to keep coming to the church although several started going elsewhere to find worship more to their taste. One day Jim was summoned by the new priest and blamed, quite unjustly, for stirring up the congregation against him. He was told to worship elsewhere.

A short time after this Jim moved to a new job in the south which thankfully avoided any further conflict. It was a sad outcome after the enjoyable years Jim had spent with the church and its choir.

CHAPTER TWENTY-THREE

All Change

In the late sixties the Labour government decided to finish with the two tier system of secondary education which needed the eleven-plus examination to separate the sheep from the goats at age eleven.

In future all pupils would attend the same school, to be called a Comprehensive.

Not all authorities agreed with this change. When Margaret Thatcher led the Conservatives back to power at the next election she made the change optional. However by then most authorities were too far down the path to comprehensive education to stop it even if they wanted to.

However some did halt the process and fifty years on some areas still have their Grammar Schools as well as Comprehensives. This is especially true of Northern Ireland which still has sixty-seven Grammar Schools, about a third of their secondary schools. In the UK the figure is nearer ten percent.

It is an unarguable truth that not all of us humans have equal scholastic abilities but Jim's view now, after experiencing both systems, is that comprehensive schools are much fairer for all.

Drawing a line below a prescribed percentage of the population by means of an examination at the age of eleven is at best a pretty unreliable method of selecting who will benefit most from higher education.

What Jim did not agree with was mixed ability classes which some educators seemed to think was a natural follow on from all pupils being in the same school. Mixing the brightest pupils with those who were not so gifted seems to him to be unkind to both.

Whatever Jim's views on the inadequacy of the two tier system he cannot deny that once he got over his initial difficulties, particularly with classroom discipline, Jim's life as a Grammar School teacher was stress free and very rewarding. If the school had not been about to switch to becoming a comprehensive he would almost certainly have stayed there for the rest of his teaching life.

He had started a recorder group and a cycle club which, besides teaching road safety and cycle maintenance, also organised time trials. He had insurance cover for the trials which on one occasion he could well have had to call on as one boy, head down to go as fast as possible, rode into the back of a lorry.

Fortunately the lorry was a low loader. Although the bike came to an abrupt stop the cyclist carried on, sliding onto the empty platform of the lorry and coming to a gentle if undignified halt with no injury to him.

I am sorry to say the same cannot be said for his bike.

Enjoyable though these out-of-school activities were, the proposals for change in his Midlands town made Jim fear for the well-being of his school. He felt that the traditional staff would struggle to cope with the changes in their teaching methods which would be necessary in educating the eighty-five percent of pupils who would have gone on to Secondary Moderns.

A further concern was that the boys' grammar school was to unite with the girls' high school, which was a good half mile away, so not only was it going to be necessary to learn to teach less able pupils but also to teach girls and cope with a split site.

Jim decided to seek employment where the change might be less of a problem.

He reasoned that a Secondary Modern (eleven-plus 'failures') adapting to higher ability pupils would be far less problematic than a dual-site Grammar School having to adapt to taking in both sexes and the full ability range.

Julia was keen to move nearer to her parents so Jim applied for a Head of Mathematics post in a secondary modern school in rural Somerset. Unlike his interview at the Grammar School this was to be a hard fought battle.

He was up against four other teachers. After they had all been interviewed by a panel of governors, senior teachers and the headmaster, they were whittled down to two, one of them being Jim.

As Jim was later told, the panel was split as to which of the two candidates to appoint and it was left to the headmaster to make the final choice.

He, like Jim, was well aware that the eleven-plus was not a reliable measuring-stick and so he had a top class who stayed on beyond the age-fifteen leaving age to take their 'O' levels and then move on to 'A' levels and hopefully to University.

Jim's experience teaching in a Grammar School tipped the balance and he was given the job.

A new small housing estate was being built on a field opposite the school and one of the houses was for sale. Jim found the builder on the site and agreed to buy the house, so when he started his teaching in the West Country his journey to school was literally just a case of crossing the road from his front garden to the school gates opposite.

Horrors!

A few years later the decision was taken to close this access off.

This meant that Jim had to walk up the road a distance of a good twenty yards to get to the new entrance and then twenty yards back to the school's front door.

This was a matter about which he protested vigorously!

It was no consolation that, after he moved many years later to live in a nearby town, the county council decided to re-open the original entrance and rubbed in salt by installing a traffic-lights controlled pedestrian crossing hence restoring Jim's original route but now made even safer.

When Jim and Julia bought their new house (for £4100, hard though that is to believe nowadays) they hit a problem in that the builder would not finish the house until he had received his payment and the building society which was buying it on Jim's behalf would not pay up until the house was finished.

In the end it was agreed that if Jim paid the required deposit, the mortgage would be approved, the builder paid, and the house finished, which really was just laying some tiles in the kitchen.

The banks would not lend money at this time so Jim and Julia begged from their families. Short term interest free loans were acquired and they managed to put together enough for the deposit of about £400. The tiles were duly laid and the sale went through.

Jim worked on the large, what were to be, front and back gardens. At this point the house was built in a field so the ground needed breaking up with a pick-axe which saw Jim stripped to the waist and sweating profusely.

One of the workmen building a new house next door commented to him

"I thought you were a teacher."

On being assured that this was indeed the case he expressed amazement that a schoolteacher could wield a pick-axe navvy style. I guess many pupils find it difficult to visualise their teachers having a normal life outside the classroom.

If you have read my book, 'Total Experience Corner', you will recall that I experienced the same reaction when I suggested that I wield a machete to chop down a banana plant.

Jim's body coped with the unaccustomed exercise and by the end of the summer holiday the garden was ready for planting out. Jim, descended from gardeners on both sides, took cuttings for the front garden from many of the shrubs that made the school grounds so attractive and stocked the vegetable garden at the rear.

The field having being liberally manured by generations of cows, the height and quality of the sprouts that winter were a sight of wonder to all who beheld them.

At this time folk had started worrying about houses being poorly insulated and so wasting energy.

One idea, which was new then, though universal now, was double glazing. Jim, taking after his father again, thought that he could do it himself and so installed an extra glass sheet inside the windows.

One unfortunate problem was that the glass steamed up between the two panes. Jim reasoned that removing the air from between them would cure this unwelcome feature.

He drilled a hole from the outside of the kitchen window surround to link up with another between the panes, applied his vacuum cleaner tube to the hole and switched on.

This clever idea proved extremely effective and the air from between the two panes was efficiently extracted.

Too efficiently!

The next moment there was a loud bang as the inside pane broke sending many dagger shaped pieces of glass flying at high speed across the kitchen.

If Julia had been there, as she so often was, the result would probably have been an inquest.

If instead the outside pane had broken it would have seen Jim cut to pieces.

Another lesson learnt and the exercise was not repeated.

Jim learnt to live with a little steaming up, though allowing some ventilation to the outside via a few more holes did help even if it reduced the efficiency of the double glazing.

The vacuum cleaner was thereafter only used for its designed purpose.

Another of Jim's good ideas was to make jam.

For once though this jam is of the edible variety, not one of his tricky situations (have you lost count?).

Anyway the procedure still caused trouble as Jim was a beginner in the art of boiling up preserves and did not realise the powerful expansion property of hot fruit, sugar and water when it boils.

He got a severe dressing down from Julia when she found the top of her pristine electric stove deep in sticky red goo.

Jim cleaned it up though, not that he was given any other choice!

Another lesson learnt and, although he has continued to make jam all his life, he makes a smaller volume of jam in a larger pan.

Sadly though he continued to get into jams of the self-inflicted variety.

CHAPTER TWENTY-FOUR

Furry Things

Becoming a teacher in his new school meant it was back to square one and Jim had to learn to cope with girls and the full ability range. Respect had again to be earned and with discipline never his strongest suit (as you know) the first year or two were not easy.

Fortunately the headmaster ran a tight ship and always supported Jim to the hilt, as did his replacement when the headmaster who had appointed Jim retired a few years later.

Jim was quite correct in his reasoning that switching to comprehensive education would be much easier for a secondary modern than for a grammar school and the change over the next five years was trouble free.

It further reinforced his opinion when some years later he returned with his son and daughter to their birthplace to find not a single teacher from the boys' grammar school was still teaching there.

As a secondary modern in the country the school reflected its surroundings.

The grounds were planted with ornamental trees and shrubs, whilst the Rural Science departments kept a small number of animals, including chickens, a pig, a goat and several sheep.

The annual sheep shearing was a day to remember as the school was assembled to watch the shearer at work.

One weekend the sheep escaped, crossed the road, and feasted on Jim's newly planted shrubs and rose-bushes.

He was not best pleased about that!

The shrubs and roses recovered and Jim stayed at the school for the rest of his career, his department growing as the school gradually became comprehensive.

Sadly this necessitated many new buildings and the loss of the animals and much of what had been almost a park.

There were several incidents over the years which Jim feels will interest you.

As TV warns you, the following involves the loss of blood and close to the loss of life, human and animal, so may upset some readers.

However be assured that none of the incidents involve a vacuum cleaner, although it does involve broken glass. It makes a change from fish!

Let's start with Jim in the science lab one lunchtime

He was cadging some de-ionised water for his car battery (do you remember those days?) when into the room rushed a boy, his wrist sending a fountain of blood a foot or more into the air.

He had been being chased by another lad and had run into the glass panel of the outside door which obviously was not safety glass as it would (hopefully) be nowadays.

He had very nearly separated his hand from the rest of his body.

The two other people in the room froze with horror.

Jim somehow kept calm, grabbed the flapping hand and, pulling it back to its normal position, stemmed the flow. He then got the lad onto the floor and the school nurse was summoned. She was a highly qualified Red Cross first aider and calmly bound the lad's wound and phoned for an ambulance.

She told Jim later that when they got to the hospital she warned the nurse that it was a very bad wound, nearly an amputation, and would need care in exposing it.

No doubt the nurse was used to minor injuries being somewhat exaggerated in their description so failed to show the necessary caution and the casualty lost considerably more of his precious gore before the tide was again stemmed.

A surgeon was summoned and the lad's hand was stitched together, though as far as Jim understands it he never regained full use of his fingers.

While we are on life threatening incidents, let's mention another, although this time Jim was not involved.

As part of their final English examination pupils had to deliver a talk about their hobbies.

One pupil, living on a farm, regarded using his father's shotgun as a hobby. He brought the gun to school to use as a visual aid to make his talk more interesting, which I am sure it would have done.

The lad gave the gun to his teacher for safe keeping.

This was probably the first, and certainly the last, time the teacher had been given a gun by a pupil. Presumably failing to realise the potential danger he put it in an unlocked cupboard to await the appointed hour of the lad's talk.

The next time he saw the gun was, however, not during the talk. Instead the pupil had crept into the room during the lunch hour and taken it to show his mates, who I am sure were mightily impressed. What his mates did not know was that the gun was loaded with shot.

No doubt thinking it would be fun to pretend to shoot his mate, one pupil put the barrel into the stomach of one of his peers and pulled the trigger.

Once again the school nurse coped calmly with this completely unexpected first-aid situation and kept the injured boy stable whilst an ambulance was summoned.

That the lad survived was down to the fact that, with the barrel of the gun close to his stomach, the shot was concentrated in a small area and he was lucky that the surgeons were able to remove most of it with no major damage to vital organs, although Jim believes the casualty bears in his body to this day some lead-shot which it was impossible to safely remove.

Finally in this round up of memorable incidents at the school we need to address the problems of rabbits (or bunnies or furry things, if you are a Portlander or Cornish fisherman).

A family of them had set up home on the school playing field, rapidly multiplying, as they do, and soon becoming an army, busily digging many burrows. The sports' teachers were concerned that pupils would trip in the holes whilst running at speed after a ball, or after another pupil, or possibly away from a teacher. They might do a mischief to their ankles or something worse to something higher up.

It was decided that the rabbits had to go.

Persuading these fast-breeders to move elsewhere by explaining the hazard they were causing and would they mind moving to another field pretty please was considered unlikely to be a success and it was decided that extermination was the only answer.

With hindsight this should have been delayed and carried out during a school holiday, but this was some months away so a local pest control firm was asked to deal with the problem as soon as possible using a lethal gas.

Somehow this plan became public knowledge and it horrified those pupils and teachers who saw rabbits as cuddly harmless innocents as presented in 'Watership Down' and 'The Tale of Peter Rabbit'. Many 'Save Our Bunnies' banners were created and a protest rally organised, to be held on the day the dastardly deed was to be carried out.

Faced with such a vociferous strength of feeling, the executioners took one look at the angry pupils, plus a few equally angry teachers, and withdrew. The slaughter was called off. Tempers cooled.

However a few weeks later there was not a rabbit to be seen on the hallowed turf.

You can make up your own explanation for this!

If you have been keeping score it is time to report on Jim's body count which now went up by one, to three.

Whilst driving his wife and young children on a day out they came upon an upturned car with a hole in its shattered windscreen and what was obviously the driver in the gutter equally obviously dead as he had exited his vehicle head first. He presumably was not wearing a seat-belt (if he had one; they were not mandatory in the UK until 1983) and must have lost control by driving too fast round the corner.

Julia did not want the children to see this unpleasant sight and insisted that Jim drove on. Hopefully the next person on the scene did report the incident but it left Jim feeling somewhat guilty that he had obeyed Julia and driven by, although it was obvious that the man was dead.

CHAPTER TWENTY-FIVE

A Vast Expense

Not long after Jim started at his new school came DC-Day, otherwise known as Decimal Currency Day: the Fifteenth of February 1971. The local business association members were very concerned as to how they were going to cope with this change when they had only known Pounds, Shillings (20 to the Pound) and Pennies (12 to the shilling, 240 to the pound) with its many coins including florins (two shillings) and half-crowns (thirty pence). Jim was asked to organise some training evenings, though he thought a quick five minutes was all that was really needed.

Plastic coins in the new denominations were obtained and a shop set up so that the shopkeepers could practise taking coins and giving the correct change.

Jim thinks that after the first ten minutes all attendees felt it was so simple that the only question was "Why did we not change years ago?"

The remaining time was spent looking at the other metric measures. The change to these has certainly not been as sudden, the old ones hanging on in there so we sometimes end up with a mixture of both, as with timber where one can buy a 2.5 (metres) length of four by four (inches!) and pounds weight is still the preferred option for new-borns, not to mention petrol sold in litres with consumption often quoted in miles per gallon.

The seventies were a time of huge change on the electronic front.

Leading the way was the hand-held calculator. Decimal currency had come in just in time, although one can only surmise how difficult it would have been to have had a Pounds, Shillings and Pence calculator.

The Japanese firm Sharp were the leaders in the field and in 1973 the first hand-held battery-powered ones came on the market. A Sharp's sale rep. drove fifty miles from Bristol to show to Jim and his headmaster one of these miracles. They cost around £100, which in 2021 would be £4000. Jim thought his school should own one and his headmaster was won over. It was such a vast expense that the school governors had to meet to approve the outlay. To their credit they agreed to indulge the school. Once the payment had been made the Sharp's rep. again drove all the way from Bristol to deliver this precious jewel.

It needed four AA batteries which lasted about an hour of continuous use and had the new technology of a liquid crystal display which was the main cause of it being so expensive. It did the four basic computations, add, subtract, multiply and divide. It had no memory or any other functions but it was a wonder of the age.

A parents' evening was arranged and the calculator was demonstrated then passed around the parents. They were mightily impressed.

The school only having just the one it did not benefit the pupils but Jim enjoyed using it and it continued to do sterling service in the school office for many years afterwards.

I wonder where it is now.

Hot on the heels of the calculator came the dawn of small (well at least not room-sized) computers and around 1974 the school received one.

Jim had first experienced the joy of Basic programming in 1959 when his college was able to book time on one of the UK's few Ferranti computers situated at Manchester University, several hundred miles away.

Having been taught the language which the computer understood he wrote a program to calculate the length of the hypotenuse of a right-angle triangle given the other two sides. Pythagoras got there first of course, but I guess in his wildest dreams he could not have envisaged a day when a machine would be able to apply his theorem.

Jim's program was typed into a tele-printer which produced a long strip of paper with punched holes encoding the numbers and letters. This was then transmitted by telephone to Manchester to be fed into their computer when they had a spare minute. A week later the result came back and, wonder of wonders, it had worked.

Jim still has the punched tape; it is a treasured possession.

Many years later he was chatting to a stranger over a coffee about his early days of computing and it turned out that the man had been one of the university staff who operated their electronic marvel and could well have been the person who fed in Jim's program.

Now though Jim was in charge of his own machine, a Research Machines 380Z. It came in a large metal box with a separate black and white display screen and used a six inch disc to save its data and its programmes.

When switched on the screen lit up (eventually) and the computer just sat there waiting to be told what to do. There were no programs (now called 'apps') available so the operator had to give it instructions in Basic. This Jim could understand. This was then electronically translated into the machine-code language which the computer could understand.

Jim found this a most enjoyable challenge and became utterly absorbed in writing programs on reams of continuous paper fed through the sprocket-driven printer. After many months and a lot of mistakes he managed to teach the computer how to provide class lists and keep a record of each pupil's test results. He also wrote a program to help the school bursar to order stationery.

This total absorption had a price though, as you will find in due course.

Things moved fast in the electronics world.

Clive Sinclair, whose transistor amplifier I told you about when Jim made his radiogram, developed a small computer called the ZX81 which was, in typical Sinclair style, tiny, especially when compared to the other computers on the market.

It was told what to do using a cassette tape recorder and needed a black and white TV to display its wonders. It boasted 48 kilobytes of operating memory (RAM) though you could boost this to 96 kilobytes with a plug in module. Unfortunately this was always coming loose and wrecking everything you had spent hours typing in.

Most modern lap tops have well over four million kb (that is 4 000 000 kb) of RAM and the laptop I am using to write this has a built in memory of 931 million kb. That is ignoring the thumbnail size memory sticks which you can plug in and which can have even vastly more than this.

Feeble by modern standards though it was, the ZX81 was a huge success, being a lot cheaper than the much larger and probably more reliable others on the market such as the BBC computer and the Commodore.

Sinclair gave the even cheaper option of buying his ZX81 in kit form and Jim soldered the components for eight of them sat at his kitchen table looking through a large magnifying lens. This would enable mathematics classes to gain some experience of these miracles.

Also a miracle was that six of them worked first time.

Mr Sinclair sorted out the other two.

Soon program tapes of games became available and Jim linked the computers together so that the same program could be loaded (if you were lucky) from just one tape recorder.

If the classroom had had a phone he might have invented the Internet but it didn't and he didn't, which is one reason amongst many why he is not the richest person on the planet, though it is not Leonard Kleinrock, who first came up with the idea in 1962, nor Tim Berners-Lee who invented the World Wide Web in 1991, but Bill Gates of Microsoft windows who has prospered on the back of the brilliant system which we now accept as just part of everyday life.

One weekend a thief broke into the school and stole all of Jim's hand-build-on-his-kitchen-table computers. They were already out of date and were later found in a river!

However the school insurance paid up and, as by then computers were improving by leaps and bounds, the Sinclair Spectrum replaced them. This used a colour TV and had the Basic language printed on the keys. It was a huge commercial success although not really suitable for much more than games playing.

That suited the pupils fine.

Jim graduated to an Acorn Archimedes, another wonder of its time, and spent yet more happy hours late into the night telling it what he wanted it to do.

In these days of Microsoft Office and the Internet it seems Jim has progressed at high speed from the Stone Age of computing to the wonder of Google being able to give answers in a split second on any question one wants answered, such as what is the time of the next train from Mombasa to Nairobi? Dr Google knows and would I like a single or a return? Dr Clever Clogs even knows how to spell Mombasa (which I didn't!).

CHAPTER TWENTY-SIX

Julie and Her Great Discovery

You now know that Jim enjoyed entertaining folk right from the days of his impromptu recitals on the bus as a toddler, so it will not surprise you to learn that he enjoyed the opportunities provided by the occasional Friday morning school assemblies.

Many of his efforts were nothing special, but Jim managed a few which he thinks were more successful.

For one of them he dusted off his conjurer's equipment, last aired when he was a teenager, and did an assembly based on 'Don't judge without knowledge. Not everything in life is what it may seem to be.'

Amongst his tricks he had a tray with a tea-pot, teacups and what appeared to be a glass jug of milk. The milk was actually Plaster of Paris with a lead weight hidden at the bottom. The jug was positioned at the inside edge of the tray so that it, cantilever style, was able to support itself and seemingly defy gravity.

At the start of his performance Jim pretended to be searching for some missing papers and, accidentally on purpose, pushed the tray over the edge of the table, much to the horror of a fellow teacher who leapt to her feet to save the whole lot hitting the floor, which of course it was not going to do.

 Hilarity all round.

 For another assembly, as Christmas drew near, he adapted a short story into a shadow play of folk coming to church with various troubles on their consciences where Jesus appeared to each troubled soul with consolation and redemption.

Some of the teaching staff were dragooned into recording the play on tape. Jim trained his pupils to act the various parts behind a large white curtain lit by a stage lamp with an overhead projector in front setting the scene.

However on the morning of the performance the leading boy acting the part of Jesus was ill and did not turn up.

Jim had to take his role.

It was not until afterwards that he realised that he had acted with his hands together in front of his trousers and when he asked one of the teachers if this was a mistake she confirmed that it had given a rather unfortunate impression when seen side on as a shadow!

Jim is quite good at sight-reading when playing the piano but has always struggled to remember any music. Take away his music score and he is lost.

He decided that he could make an assembly around this on the theme of 'Never say that you cannot do something until you have tried to do it'.

Over the next months he must have driven Julia to distraction by playing his chosen piece over and over again until he found that indeed he could play it without the music in front of him. The piece he chose, Mendelssohn's Rondo Capriccioso, was a favourite of the Head of History.

Came the day of the assembly and Jim pontificated that one should never say that you cannot do something until you have at least tried. He explained that he was going to do something that he had always believed he could not do, that is, remember a piece of music.

He launched into the quite long piece.

About half way through he mistakenly went back to an earlier part of it and repeated quite a large section. Fortunately when he again reached the spot where he had had a Groundhog Day moment he managed to get it right and successfully reached the end.

Anyone who did not know the piece well would not have noticed his error but the History teacher did and as he told Jim it caused him no little anxiety, visualising the assembly either setting an all-time record for its length with Jim possibly Groundhogging to this day, or else it would come to an abrupt and very un-Mendelssohn-y sudden end.

Jim had always enjoyed writing and in the 1980's thought up a brilliant idea for a mathematics revision book which he managed to convince a nearby educational publisher to market.

Unfortunately the rest of the mathematics teachers in the country did not find it as brilliant as Jim thought it was. It did not sell well and it was never reprinted.

However it did not put him off the notion that he could write a better maths textbook series than the ones his school was using at the time and he put his ideas to his first publishers. Perhaps not surprisingly, having had their fingers (and toes) burnt already, they were not prepared to go along with his proposal and it seemed sensible to forget it.

That Jim did not accept at this point that he was deluded was thanks to Julie, one of his pupils.

Once calculators became cheap enough to have a supply for a class his pupils needed instruction in how to use them. Calculators had come on by leaps and bounds since the highly expensive first ones but, as Jim explained, they were not much use outside the decimal system. This left a problem with time.

Napoleon (the French Emperor, not Captain Mainwaring) wanted to see time decimalised; 100 seconds to the minute and 100 minutes to the hour and 10 hours to the day perhaps, although God's decision to make a year 365 days and a bit would have caused a problem.

Napoleon won many battles.

He lost this one and later on a few more besides.

The problem Jim set was to give the arrival times of the next six buses that ran every 40 minutes, starting from 8:45.

That is assuming the bus is not the one that goes from Axminster to Weymouth and Jim is not the conductor! See Chapter Fifteen.

Jim explained that you could not do this on a calculator by keying in 845+40 as this gave the wrong answer (885).

His pupils duly tried it and agreed it did not work. All except for Julie who said it did.

"No it doesn't." said Jim.

"Yes, it does, sir." said Julie, "All you do is keep adding 40 until you get something that looks like a time."

Jim tried it. By golly, she was right!

Julie was thrilled to be teaching sir something that he did not know and she and her best friend Donna helped Jim investigate. The bell went for lunch and the class left, but the two girls stayed on whilst they tested things out. They found it works fine but only for adding 20 minutes or 40 minutes and no others. They then took a late lunch.

Jim spent the weekend writing this up and sent his article to the

Times Educational Supplement under the title of 'Julie and Her Great Discovery'.

The article ended *'Maybe Julie's great discovery will not go down the ages alongside Pythagoras's Theorem and Archimedes' Principle but I am sure Julie's elation equalled that felt by either of these personages. Suddenly the story of Archimedes dripping along the streets of Syracuse crying "Eureka!" when he discovered in his bath how to work out how to find out if the king's crown was indeed gold seems a lot more credible, although Julie would no doubt have done it a lot more daintily.'*

A few days later he received a phone call from the TES editor to tell him that his article was to be published. "You'll need to edit it first." suggested Jim, only to be told that they were not going to change a single word.

That did Jim's morale and confidence a power of good.

When his article graced the front page his headmaster had it framed and displayed it on his wall.

If Jim had chosen a bus service running every fifteen minutes Julie would not have made her discovery and Jim maybe would never have re-found his self-belief which was never strong. However he had luckily chosen a forty minutes timetable, Julie arrived in The Times Educational Supplement and, confidence somewhat restored, Jim sent his plan for a new maths book series to other firms.

One in Exeter took the bait.

As with his early days of computing, Jim devoted every spare moment to writing his books. Then one day, the initial drafts for the set of five pupils' and five teachers' books being ready, a letter came from the Exeter publishers informing him that the firm had been taken over by another company and their new owners were not prepared to publish his work.

Oh No!

CHAPTER TWENTY-SEVEN

Jim In The Steps Of Byron (But Far Behind)

Sometimes what seems like a disaster turns out to be a god-send and this was the case with Jim's text-books.

He attended a teachers' conference which was addressed by an author of a book on the teaching of mathematics whose thoughts and ideas were very close to Jim's. In the lunch hour he chatted to her and told her the sad tale of his aborted text-book publication.

She told him that her publisher, John Murray, was looking to publish a maths textbook series and she would mention it to them.

Things moved very fast from then on. Jim received a phone call to arrange a meeting in London and, after the manuscripts were sent for review, he was given the green light, although not without some major changes to the books which much improved them.

However it meant Jim had to spend many more hours doing the necessary rewriting.

Computers in those days were not very good at producing maths books so the work was all done on a typewriter with a carbon paper copy. These pages were then sent to a printer who produced reams of paper with continuous text, called a galley.

An artist was employed to produce the many diagrams and then the galley text and the diagrams were physically cut into small pieces and pasted up, using 'cow gum', to make the final format of each page which the printer then used to typeset them ready for printing.

Cow gum is named after the company who invented it, F.P. Cow; nothing to do with mooing creatures. It is petroleum based and, whilst tacky when applied, takes a long time to dry fully, so an editor can move the pieces around for some while until satisfied.

Jim, telling me of cow gum, was reminded of the traditional wood glue which his father heated on the gas stove. This was indeed made from the hooves of cows and other ungulates. Apparently it smells something terrible.

This 'cut and paste' job would be carried out by an employee at the publishers. It is a time-consuming activity which Jim got to know intimately because of yet another of his all too common unfortunate 'jams'.

Book One was due to be published in the following May and the publisher had been promoting it like mad. Then one day, not long before the finished paste-ups were due at the printers, came a phone call from London.

The employee who was given the 'cut and paste' job had had a nervous breakdown and was in hospital. When his office was visited to obtain what was expected to be the nearly complete pages it was found that nothing had been done past Page Three. It seemed that all the while it was assumed that he was working on the book he was in such a depressed state that he could not work and had presumably just sat there in his misery staring at the wall.

Jim knows the feeling.

The commissioning editor told Jim that they were in deep trouble. The finished pages were due at the printer in ten days' time and a huge investment looked likely to go down the pan.

Jim, cheeky fellow that he is, told him that there was no reason why he could not do the job himself.

Although I am sure that his editor was extremely doubtful that Jim could indeed do what he thought he could do, he had little to lose by letting him try, so Jim was brought the artwork, galleys and tins of cow-gum and he set to work.

Although very short of sleep he got the first book laid out in time to meet the printer's deadline. The effects of inhaling the cow-gum fumes may have helped!

He was later told that he had cost the publisher 'an arm and a leg' with the way he had split up the text but it turned out well in the end as the books sold at high speed and were reprinted many times.

Jim was entrusted with the cut and paste job on the next two as well!

Occasionally that boy does well!

In his early seventies Jim's dad had a heart attack while he was visiting Julia & Jim.

In those days there was no treatment such as stents or by-pass surgery, so if one's heart survived the initial blockage the only treatment was rest and no demanding manual labour.

Julia did all the right things; a doctor and an ambulance was summoned. Jim's dad pulled through.

As you know he was never one to be idle so spent his last precious years continuing to observe his philosophy of being able to do anything another man can do by making marquetry pictures, cross-stitch tapestries, inlaid wooden gifts for his grandchildren and his piece de resistance, a violin which has a superb tone and is treasured by his descendants.

As the years of recuperation went by he started on more challenging tasks. The last of which was after his car failed its MOT. It needed a new exhaust and Jim's 'I can do anything you can do better' dad was soon lying on the road under his jacked-up car in the middle of February.

He succeeded in fitting the part but it was more than his weakened heart could cope with and, a week later, just short of his 79th birthday, he passed into the care of God, no doubt still finding something in Paradise that needed his 'Mr Fix-it' skills.

A full and productive life, even if darkened by much sadness and the untimely loss of a daughter and a grand-daughter.

Jim's mum lived on for another twenty years, for much of it in a 'granny flat' in Jim's sister's house. She was the kindest person imaginable and much loved by all who came to know her.

Her life with Jim's dad had its ups and downs as all marriages must, but they were generally happy together. When things got tough his dad went for a long walk and, as you know, his mum got out the secateurs.

She had a sister who lived in a house overlooking the Isle of Portland and, on a good day, a beautiful view it certainly was.

However one afternoon while the family were there celebrating a birthday, a sea mist had come down and Jim's mum uttered the memorable instruction: "Come! Look at Portland! You can't see it!"

This is a source of much amusement to all who remember her.

The i-paper managed something of the same sort in 2021 when it ran a feature on the May 'blood moon' with a long explanation of what this is and how it was caused. Having thus whetted its readers' appetite to observe this phenomenon it added, at the end of the article, a footnote explaining that we in the UK would not be able to observe it anyway as we were round the wrong side of the world during the time it occurred.

I guess all families have such remembered phrases as Jim's

mum's instruction to look at an island that could not be seen, most of which only mean anything to those with intimate knowledge of how they arose.

Another one which would mean nothing to anyone else was "I'll start the engine, you take the oars." which arose when Jim and his dad were in a boat with his angler uncle (he of the weather-fish) in Portland Harbour when a destroyer was suddenly observed coming straight for them at speed.

An 'I'll start the engine; you take the oars' moment is when one has suddenly found oneself in a dodgy situation, possibly at dire risk to life or at least to limb.

Starting the engine proved somewhat difficult but frantic rowing and maybe an observant destroyer captain saw Jim and his fellow seafarers safely through.

I started to tell you of Jim's mum's life after his dad died and seem to have been side-tracked yet again.

She made the most of her last years. She had much talent as a water-colour painter, mainly of birds and flowers. She painted many cards and larger works of art, all beautifully executed.

Sadly, as with her mother and two of her three sisters, senile dementia took hold in her nineties and she spent the last two years in a care home where she seemed very contented and was again much loved. Jim was able to visit often and take her for a drive.

In her last months she could no longer recognise Jim but the last time she did realise who he was she commented "I do so love you, Jim" which is a memory he will always treasure.

CHAPTER TWENTY-EIGHT

Breaking Up Is Hard To Do

Jim and Julia acquired a taste for continental holidays, usually as a couple, with their children staying with their grandparents.

The first of these was to Sicily in the summer holidays which proved to be an inadvisable time to go as it was unbearably hot as they toured Greek temple after Greek temple, always needing a climb up a hill and, to Jim's untutored eyes, one temple looking very little different to any other.

However they did discover the beautiful town of Taormina to which they returned for a longer stay another year. The Greek theatre there has a backdrop of Mount Etna. Performances are still staged so Jim & Julia hired a cushion each and sat on the stone steps to enjoy a show.

The beach, many metres below the town, is also beautiful as, so Jim discovered to his delight, were the topless female sun worshippers.

Other holidays were also spent in Italy. One week they stayed in Rome and caught the slow, very slow, train to Naples on the Tuesday to have a look round Pompeii.

They had carefully checked that Pompeii was only closed to the public on a Monday, so were nonplussed when on arriving there they were met with the sign 'Chioso' (closed).

It turned out that because of a Saints' Day holiday it had opened specially on the Monday and so the staff were taking Tuesday off instead.

Having spent all morning on the train, Jim and Julia decided to see what they could see without a guide and found a way in round the back. It was not where the tourists were taken but it was interesting, although they were spotted in the distance by some security guards who yelled at them. They had to run for it before they found themselves in a Neapolitan jail accused of trespass.

Whilst in Rome Jim saw an advertisement in the paper for a teacher of mathematics in an 'English' school in the city. As, like so many holiday-makers, to both of them the foreign clime seemed far preferable to that of England, Jim decided to apply.

He duly wrote to the headmaster, found out the price of a stamp, and posted his application in a nearby letter-box. About a month after Jim and Julia had returned home a letter came from the Rome headmaster. He was sorry to inform Jim that his application letter had taken three weeks to cross Rome and by the time it did arrive the vacancy had been filled by someone else.

With hindsight Jim thinks this is probably just as well, although he still loves Italy and its often laid-back people.
Jim and Julia also returned to Rudesheim, where Jim had been on his prize holiday with the escapee wives, and spent a week on the Greek Island of Kos, where they were able one day to swim in a mountain lake under a waterfall; 'au naturel'. This was not entirely by choice as they had not brought their swim-wear but the water was so inviting!

You have read of Jim's obsessions with computers and his authorship of maths textbooks, so it will probably come as no surprise to you that his marriage suffered.

Jim did find time to play the piano for his daughter's ballet classes and he taught his children and his wife to drive, somewhat of a cheek when he had not ever had a driving lesson himself.

However with her son and daughter growing up and becoming independent and her husband always busy, Julia felt, not unjustifiably, unwanted and neglected.

She met a man who seemed to need her more than her husband did and one Sunday morning she left to make a start on carving out a new life for herself.

Jim was distraught, became profoundly depressed, and for nine months was unable to concentrate on his writing or much else.

Julia too found that she was torn between her husband and her new man so the break-up was far from clean.

After nearly two years she submitted divorce papers and remarried.

The good news is that Jim and Julia have remained on friendly terms to this day and when Jim remarried some time later the four met up for the occasional meals.

After he retired from his stone-masonry employment at sixty-five, Julia's dad would prove the beneficial effect of fresh air and exercise, plus having good genes.

He loved being out in the open, walking several miles around Portland most days. He took up bowls, kept his garden going, and always welcomed Jim and his second wife with a mug of tea when they visited him through the years ahead, for indeed there were many years ahead for him.

At his 100th birthday he took to the stage and sang to entertain his many guests, then kept going for another four years before eventually Father Time caught up with him. He had started writing poetry soon after Jim met Julia and kept this up all his life, having several published volumes to his name.

He was a lovely man.

◆ ◆ ◆

Back to the last days of Jim's and Julia's marriage. After nine-months spent hoping that Julia would come back to him it came to New Year's Day and Jim decided that he had to face facts and start making a new life for himself. He joined Nexus, an organisation for singles and in these pre-internet days also responded to and met a few women who had advertised in the local paper's 'lonely hearts' column.

This led to a few friendships and some highly memorable 'one-night stands' but he did not meet anyone who he felt he wanted to make a new life with, although he did seriously consider proposing to one of the Nexus club's single ladies who he went to dancing classes with for over a year.

She flattered Jim by working through his first maths text book and she was sold on the idea of them buying a local high-street shop. If this had become a reality Jim would have been following in his parent's and great-grandparent's foot-steps.

Somehow the spark with his dance partner did not seem to be there and the relationship remained platonic, even the tango failing to provide the excitement it promises.

Being now somewhat less in mental anguish Jim managed to start on the rewrite of the final book in his text-book series with the valued support and encouragement of his sister and a female older cousin who lived in Northern Ireland.

On reflection he wonders if the cousin, whose husband had died suddenly in his fifties, saw Jim as a potential future partner. Although they had a few enjoyable holidays together and had much in common, including an addiction to cryptic crossword puzzles, romance never blossomed.

CHAPTER TWENTY-NINE

Dancing Girls

The builder who he had met on the day of his interview had a fatal heart-attack a few years before Jim was divorced. His widow became a cook at the school. Knowing that Jim was alone she suggested that he might like to come with her to a weekly singles dance in Yeovil. This Jim did. He had no interest in a relationship with the builder's widow but he did meet and take out a few other ladies.

Many of the dances were 'progressive' so that all the singles met all the others and one evening Jim found himself dancing with a lady who very much appealed to him, though he thought her far too young to ask out.

Two weeks later she came again and they chatted together when not dancing and found that they had many common likes and dislikes. Her name was Stephanie and she worked in the pharmacy at the local Mental Hospital.

Jim asked if she would like to come to a symphony concert, an offer which she accepted, and the friendship blossomed.

Stephanie had been invited to the singles dance club by a nurse at the hospital who she remained friends with until the nurse's death many years' later. Jim thinks she was grateful to her!

When Jim looks at photos of Stephanie taken when they first met he can see why he thought her far too young for him, for she looks to be in the first blush of youth, but it turned out that she was nearly four years older than he was, so her age was not a barrier to them getting to know each other with both perhaps considering the possibility of setting up home together.

◆ ◆ ◆

Let's spend a while hearing about Stephanie's previous life.

On leaving her girls' High School in the West Midlands Stephanie had trained as a Pharmaceutical Dispenser. On completing her course at the second try (a co-incidence that she shared with a famous writer which I will tell you about later) she was invited by an aunt, who had emigrated, to join her in Canada and take a job there.

This Stephanie did and when the local paper got to hear of her plan they interviewed her, producing a feature in their women's section under the headline 'Dudley Girl Off to a New Life in Canada.' For the next year Stephanie worked in a chemist's shop in Toronto, writing two very long letters describing her life in Canada, both of which were again given pride of place as articles in the paper. The first of these had the headline 'A Dream Trip to a New World.'

She might well have stayed far across the pond for the rest of her life, but during the course of that year her father, only in his early fifties, became seriously ill with lung problems, probably silicosis from breathing in asbestos dust at his work.

Stephanie returned home and a few weeks later her father died. She was only twenty-one and like many daughters worshipped her dad so it was a terrible blow.

She supported her mother through this sad time and found work in a local hospital. After a few years her mother re-married and Stephanie was free to make friendships of her own.

She had no problems finding male companions and it seemed to Jim later in their life together that she was rather like a sailor with a girl in every port as wherever they went Stephanie would have been there before, with Philip or John or Richard or Tom, or Dick, or Harry, or a lover she always called 'dear dear Robert'.

Some of these were still married; others seemed not interested in being tied down.

One of her beaux owned a motorised glider and took her to France. Her job was to navigate, a skill not taught to a pharmacist and she belonged to the brigade who have to turn a road map upside down if one is travelling south in order to work out whether the next turn is a right one or a left one.

This is not a huge problem on terra firma. It is somewhat more life threatening when up in the skies. There was some panic as Stephanie had to admit that she had no idea where they were and they could not find the destination airfield, though I guess any airfield where they could land would have done. The pilot did eventually find one and being a glider there probably was not too big a problem if they ran out of fuel, assuming that they could find any large open space.

Whether the friendship survived Jim does not know. He does know that Stephanie's flight home was her last experience of being in a glider.

In her early forties, Stephanie did receive a proposal and married. Sadly the marriage was not a happy one and they soon parted, divorcing after the no-blame two year separation period.

Around the same time her mother's second husband died and Stephanie again found herself with a distraught mother to care for. Not for long as her mother, no doubt grief stricken at the loss of two husbands, also died.

Stephanie bravely decided to make a fresh start and was successful in being given the job in Somerset. In one of the many co-incidences with which she seemed to have a Dickensian familiarity, when she arrived in the hospital pharmacy on her first day who should be there but a colleague she had been friends with in her Midlands pharmacy. The friend had left there to marry after which they had lost touch. This friendship blossomed again and lasted through the years ahead.

In co-incidence number two, and counting, Jim had a cousin living up north in the same town as the one where her father had grown up and where several of Stephanie's cousins still lived so they went there for their first holiday together and had a cousin-fest.

Stephanie also took Jim to view a local stately home, Astley Hall. This mansion was built in the 1600's and was lived in by the Charnock family. It has been much extended over the years but with the upkeep needing more finance than the last inhabitant, not a Charnock, could support, it was in the 1920's gifted to the town council.

According to one of Stephanie's aunts, whose mother was indeed a Charnock, her family was descended from this wealthy family whose most famous son was Job Charnock.

Job was the founder of Calcutta; at least he was according to the English who set up trading posts in India known as The East India Company.

Job was indeed a relative of the Lancashire Charnock family although the Calcutta authorities do not accept him as the founder of their city, having proof that there was a settlement there long before Job came on the scene.

What is certain is that he was a very successful businessman and his life story needs a book of its own (watch this space!) but his contemporaries found him a 'silent morose man'. This may be sour grapes as he had made himself unpopular by stamping out the smuggling which was endemic amongst them.

He took as a 'common law wife' a widow who was one of the native population, though rumours that he 'rescued' her from her Indian husband's funeral pyre are probably just gossip.

He renamed his wife Maria and with her he had a son and three daughters, or possibly four daughters, or even an unknown number of children; the records are somewhat foggy, but apparently his daughters all married well.

During a holiday in India Jim and Stephanie visited Job's mausoleum in Calcutta which he built for Maria when she died and very impressive it is too, so he must have loved her very much.

Was Stephanie a descendant of Job's daughters? Although Stephanie spent some time on researching her ancestral tree she could not find a direct link to the Charnocks of Astley Hall. However she had a firm belief that the mansion had once been owned by a member of her family and that there was 'money in Chancery' awaiting proof of entitlement to ownership, though this is tenuous in the extreme.

However it gave Jim much pleasure to tease her about her delusions of grandeur and they always visited their family mansion and discussed its upkeep on their annual trips 'up north'.

Around this time Jim decided to take his form group by coach to London to see the sights and take in an ice show. As usual he was skating on thin ice himself.

Part of the experience for these country teenagers was to go on a tube train. They left Westminster on the Jubilee line heading for Bond Street. The tube was busy and his class got a little separated. At the first stop, Green Park, Jim was horrified see several boys leaving the train. He had not told his class that their journey involved more than one stop. Too late, the tube was already on its way.

Again, oh for a mobile phone.

When Jim and the rest of his class reached the theatre the missing boys were there waiting for their classmates.

Jim thought it best not to enquire too deeply into how they had spent the time nor how they had managed to make their own way to the theatre.

CHAPTER THIRTY

Love Is Wonderful The Second Time Around

When Jim met Stephanie she was living in the nurses' quarters at the Wells Mental Hospital but, as she was a pharmaceutical dispenser, she had no rights to be a resident there and was being pressured to find her own accommodation. Jim suggested that she take out a mortgage on a flat, which she did.

Understandably she was not happy at the prospect of living in the same house as had Jim and Julia. It seemed that, if they were to make a life together, Jim would have to move. He did not mind leaving the house. He was very sorry to have to leave his garden.

One day a colleague of Jim's at school told him that she was selling her Edwardian terraced house which Jim had once visited and much admired.

"I will buy it." Jim responded, much to her surprise.

A valuation was agreed; Jim sold his house opposite the school and moved in. Jim named the house Astley Cottage in honour of Stephanie's (wishful thinking) stately home up north.

A year or two later Stephanie sold her flat, making a handsome profit, and she moved in with Jim after she had taken him to the Peter Pan statue in Kensington Gardens so that he could propose to her in front of it. He did not need much persuasion.

On another trip to London Jim took Stephanie to his John Murray publishers, an experience she loved. It was still based in the second John Murray's house where the upstairs drawing room had been kept as it was in Lord Byron's day, together with his gloves and other items and a painting of him above the very fireplace in which the two volumes of Byron's intimate hand-written memoires were burnt after his death to avoid a scandal. Given what we now know of Byron's life, it seems that folk who knew him filled in the gaps, and when one reads a biography of him one can see why his publisher was concerned.

Shortly after this visit to London a notice went up on the teachers' common-room notice board advertising The League of Commonwealth Teachers which was looking for teachers who would exchange for a year with a Commonwealth one. With Jim's writing no longer demanding all his attention and with the introduction of the National Curriculum being a huge worry he thought a year in a different country was tempting. Stephanie had fallen in love with India on a holiday spent on the Maharajah's Express Train tour so was all for it and Jim applied.

On his interview at The League it was thought that he would not cope with the Indian languages so the Caribbean was suggested as a better option. The year in the Caribbean was a great adventure although he does not know if his mum was amused or horrified by the letters he wrote to her describing his adventures, but the team at the League apparently always knew their boss had received a letter from Jim by the peals of laughter coming from her office as she read of his frustrations and adventures. Jim's jams were international.

Stephanie, as I have said, really only agreed to the exchange because of her love affair with India (and with an Indian doctor – another one of the many beaux in her life). She said that she would have married him but his mother would not allow it and, truth to tell, Jim thinks she would have struggled to be a dutiful wife when, as he planned to do, he returned to work in India.

With its very different social attitudes and its poverty, not to mention its climate, she would all too soon have 'married in haste and repented at leisure'.

However his fiancée was not going to let Jim go abroad for a year on his own, probably very wisely, so she accepted it would have to be the Caribbean, not India, where she would spend the following year. In setting up the exchange it was explained that, as only Jim would have employment there, Stephanie could be sent home after her six-month visa expired. This would not apply if they were married and so, although marriage was certainly planned in the next few years, it seemed best to marry before they set off.

So they did, on one of the hottest days of the century.

Jim has never had any regrets.

He spent his 'stag night' sat in his very hot car in a station car-park waiting for hours for his son to arrive from university. Like his parents' oven buying fiasco it was yet another time when mobile phones would have come in useful but the widespread use of these was still a good few years away. The heat had affected the rails and the points and so trains were running many hours late, having to wait for the sun to go down and for things to cool off a little.

Stephanie had a life-long passion for classical music, being a regular Albert Hall proms-goer including, before she met Jim, several 'Last Nights'. Rachmaninoff was her all-time favourite, both his life story and his music. Jim had a rival. Fortunately his wife was only able to have a passionate affair with him in her mind.

She joined the Rachmaninoff Society and was elected to its committee. She and Jim spent several holidays in the steps of the master; to Russia, to his villa in Switzerland and, whilst visiting Jim's niece in New York, to his and his daughter's grave in Kensico Cemetery, Valhalla, a hamlet forming part of New York City. I am sure Wagner would have approved of a fellow composer passing eternity in Valhalla, home of the gods of his Ring Cycle. In fact the hamlet was so named in honour of Wagner by a fan of the maestro.

On the same holiday, which was in mid-winter, they visited Niagara Falls which was deep in snow with wonderful ice crystals decorating the trees. Apart from two Japanese busy taking photos Jim and Stephanie had Niagara Falls to themselves.

Not many people can say that.

Other holidays were spent in touring Jim's eloping ancestor's Ireland three times and loving it each visit for its stunning scenery and friendly people. They also went twice to the Channel Isles, had a round Britain cruise, went three times to Italy, sailed to Norway on the QE2 (just once, in its final year before becoming a floating Hotel in Dubai), and visited friends and relations in Australia, coming home via a week in the South Seas' Cook Islands.

This last holiday also included an unscheduled stop in Tahiti as one of the plane's engines was giving trouble. Jim and Stephanie spent a whole night in the departure lounge with, due to the plane being parked right outside the lounge windows, a perfect view of the faulty engine being examined and, they hoped, being successfully repaired by some engineers. Good news; it worked OK the next day!

A long weekend in Paris saw Jim causing his tour leader a minor problem when he fell for a scam which the internet tells me is very common in the city and has spread to other tourist destinations across Europe. Jim and his tour group were walking along the banks of the Seine when a chap coming the other way picked up what appeared to be a gold ring and handed it to Jim. Jim did not know what to do with it but having looked at it hung onto it. A few minutes later the tour guide came to him and asked if Jim has been given a ring.

Jim said that yes he had. The guide said he had to give it back which of course he did and the scammer was 'bought off' from giving any more trouble with a few cigarettes.

You may wonder what all that was about and so does Jim. According to the internet the idea usually is to offer to sell the gullible tourist the fake ring in exchange for some cash. As far as Jim knows the scammer had not offered to sell the ring to him but then you may remember he failed to pass French 'O' level three times so maybe his assailant did ask for money and Jim did not understand.

All very strange, but if you find yourself in Paris some day do watch out.

Jim and Stephanie also booked two coach tours in the States which led to yet another addition to Stephanie's list of coincidences. On the first of these tours, a fortnight touring Arizona, they much enjoyed the company and humour of Lon, their courier, who lived in that State. Amazingly when they got back Stephanie discovered that her card-making-club teacher had been on the same holiday with Lon two weeks' earlier. Not perhaps such a dramatic coincidence but the next one certainly was.

Several years' later Jim and Stephanie booked a coach tour of the Great Lakes, not with the same company and of course on the other side of the USA to Arizona. When they reached Chicago airport they heard a voice that they thought they recognised. It can't be, can it? But round the corner came their Arizona guide, Lon.

Although the tour was organised by a company Lon had not worked for in the past, it turned out that the guide who was booked to look after them had gone sick.

Lon, being found on a database of guides and being available, had been flown in from Arizona to take his place.

All three of them being amazed at this unexpected turn of events, they felt destiny was giving them a message so, after another two great and much enjoyed weeks together ('Great Lakes, Great Holiday'), they promised to keep in touch and have done so to this day.

CHAPTER THIRTY-ONE

Another Great Escape

Jim had not long been back from his Caribbean experience when another notice went up on the staffroom notice board. This time it was from the County Council explaining that they were very sorry but they were unable to fund all the existing teachers' salaries for the coming year and they wondered if any teacher who was over fifty years old would mind taking their full pension immediately rather than hang on until they had taught the required forty years.

Was that a stampede you have just witnessed, all heading for the headmaster's door?

"Me! Me!" was the cry.

Jim was not lead bull but he wasn't far behind.

Because his second-in-the-department had run it very efficiently while Jim was in the Caribbean he persuaded his headmaster to agree that he could apply for the new deal as he would be leaving the department in very capable and proven good hands. An application was put in and a few months later Jim retired at the grand old age of fifty-four.

Jim would not be idle in his retirement though. The school matron saw to that. She pounced on Jim and with a slight twist of his arm persuaded him that he could make a new life for himself by joining her beloved Red Cross. This he did and so began twenty-six years of voluntary service and counting.

One of his first tasks was to take on organising the local blood donation sessions. This involved firstly advertising the sessions, then greeting and checking in the donors, as well as organising a team of volunteers to serve the traditional cup of tea after the blood had been taken. He also presented the awards given after ten, twenty-five, and fifty donations.

Jim himself got to losing his fifty, plus a few, 'armfuls' before he reached the cut off age as it was in those days.

The local Red Cross team was very small and had no building of their own. However there was a large group of first aiders in the nearest big town so Jim joined this team and on Monday evenings during the next year learnt all the skills necessary to help casualties survive. Having passed his final exam he began helping out as a first-aider at local events.

Of course, Jim being Jim, he soon decided that he was just as able to teach volunteers about the Red Cross and how to perform first aid as the existing teachers and he has so done until this day.

At least he has no discipline problems teaching first aid to adults. Just gets his chest pummelled.

Here we come to the fourth, and final (I hope) of Jim's intimate experiences with death.

He and Stephanie went to Sidmouth for some sea air and to indulge Stephanie in her favourite activity of shopping.

Walking up the main street they came upon a small group of people and saw an elderly man sat in a shop doorway in very obvious distress. Jim pushed through, announcing that he was a first aider. Having checked that an ambulance was on its way he turned his attention to the casualty.

It soon became obvious that the man was having a heart attack and it was not long before he lost consciousness and stopped breathing. For the first and (so far) only time in his life Jim had to put into practice for real the hundreds of times he had shown people how to try to save the life of a plastic mannequin.

Ignoring the advice of the onlookers to 'wait for the ambulance' Jim knew that he had to move fast and was soon carrying out the procedures he had so often taught others to do.

Shortly afterwards the ambulance turned up.

'Relief, I shall be able to let them take over.' he thought.

Not a chance.

"You seem to know what you are doing, sir. Please keep going."

The paramedic fixed an airway to the man so that air could be given without the need for the mouth-to-mouth resuscitation which Jim had been doing. Jim kept pumping his chest to try to persuade the man's heart to keep the brain supplied with oxygenated blood.

The man was carried into the ambulance where he was wired up to the electrocardiograph and the defibrillator was brought into action.

Sadly, though given my introduction to this section probably coming as no shock to you, the man's heart showed no electrical activity and after several attempts it was decided that the old man had gone to join the angels.

Jim is sorry. He really did try his best.

The ambulance crew took the man to hospital where he could be formally pronounced dead whilst Jim re-joined Stephanie for a much needed mug of strong tea to help him recover both mentally and physically from his experience.

Although a rapid start of CPR and the use of a defibrillator can and does save lives, it is by no means a certainty that it will work in spite of the fact that it always seems to in fictional presentations on television.

This was one of the times that it does not have the desired effect.

◆ ◆ ◆

A year or so after Jim became a volunteer he found that there was another Red Cross volunteer unit in the next village that had a small building, called a Centre, and this had for many years opened on a Thursday morning serving hot drinks in return for a donation. They also sold donated goods like a Charity Shop.

Most importantly though it provided a venue, company, and friendship for local folk, including many pensioners, to meet and exchange tales of successes, or woes.

It seemed sensible to combine the two groups, their villages being only four miles apart.

The Centre leader was looking to retire having been very active for many years including, whilst Jim was still an infant, all through the war.

Jim offered to take on her role which he is still doing until this day.

Over the next few years more volunteers were enrolled so that the Centre could open every morning except Sunday and it has become a much loved and valued addition to the facilities available to the local population.

Jim collected round him a first-aid team who he trained. Their first aid duties continued for many years, including becoming the county's first-aiders at all their athletics events.

Whilst athletics was something that Jim was no good at when at school, and sport in general had not featured largely in his life, he found athletics turned out to be very watchable and enjoyable. It was good especially to see so many youngsters taking part, giving their all to throw further, jump higher, or run faster than their peers.

So different to the media's picture of drug taking, fag smoking youths lounging in back streets and generally causing a nuisance.

Besides athletics meetings the team also covered local fetes, fairs, runs, horse rides, and so on. The horse rides did lead to a couple of veterinary services, highly unofficially. A horse with a wound on its front leg was bandaged up, whilst another was treated for a wasp sting!

They were however never asked to provide cover at the popular nudist week at a nearby open-air facility, although with his time in some exotic 'clothes optional' Caribbean hotels Jim would have fitted in, cover or no;. He is not sure about the rest of his team though.

The many different duties brought in good income for his group until the Red Cross decided to leave first aid duties to other organisations in 2019. This unexpected decision was a blow but there was good reason as, although the first aiders were all volunteers, the infrastructure needed to support them was a huge drain on the charity's finances.

Raising funds for the Red Cross led to Jim being in an exalted position when he found that a well-known conductor and television presenter lived only a few miles from his home. Jim got in touch with him and he agreed to conduct a fund-raising concert performed by the talented youngsters of two local schools. The nearby cathedral was booked for the event, which was well supported.

Jim took to the pulpit and, accustomed as he was to public speaking, delivered a sermon on the activities of the Red Cross in his area.

Afterwards there was a reception for the participants and, as Stephanie never forgot, the conductor, a lovely man, kissed her first on one cheek, and then again on the other one. Facial cheeks that is of course.

CHAPTER THIRTY-TWO

Que Sera Sera

Soon after Jim's retirement Stephanie saw an appeal in a local paper for folk interested in twinning their town with another one in Italy. She suggested that this might suit Jim and so he went to the meeting where, never one for holding back, he offered to be their treasurer.

This led to a whole new raft of experiences.

Although Jim does not share in any way his daughter's ability to speak a foreign tongue, he gets by when the two nationalities meet up, with the aid of a phrase book and a lot of gesturing, the latter being a must for the Italians themselves when conversing.

You may be wondering what jams this will get our Jim into. I will not have to disappoint you!

Jim decided that one visit of the group should start with a few days on the Northern Italian coast. That went smoothly but, in trying to be helpful, he assisted the Italian coach driver with loading the luggage. One suitcase was much heavier than Jim anticipated. He felt a twinge but carried on and they reached their twinning town where he and Stephanie settled in for their long weekend with a local schoolmistress and her husband.

The next morning Jim could not move without suffering excruciating pain. Even lying still was painful. A doctor was summoned and he provided Jim's hostess with a hypodermic syringe to administer a strong pain killer into Jim's bare backside.

This she seemed quite happy to do and indeed did so several times over the next few days.

By the time their visit was up Jim was numbed enough to make it home, using a wheel chair in Italy and chauffeur-driven disabled transport at Heathrow.

He recovered and somehow he has ever after had an especially warm close friendship with his Italian hostess.

Great oaks from little acorns grow and this certainly applies to Jim's next path to an unforeseen destination.

It all started when the twinning committee thought that their English members would undoubtedly enjoy Italian operas. Jim had been a frequent visitor to Bristol Hippodrome and had enjoyed many shows there over the years. He has particularly warm memories of a production of Hair when the dome was opened and 'petals' fell like snowflakes onto the audience below.

The Welsh National Opera made, and hopefully will continue to make, twice yearly visits to Bristol. They gave Jim many exciting and moving evenings including the whole Ring cycle.

WNO also provided a couple of memorable slip-ups, for once, or rather twice, this time not through any fault of Jim.

During a production of Orpheus in the Underworld a piece of scenery was lowered at the wrong time, coming down slowly and gently exactly over the head of Orpheus who, unlike the audience, was blissfully unaware of the descent and must have been very puzzled as to why the audience suddenly found his aria so amusing. At least it is a comic opera so it just added to the general hilarity.

Rather more unfortunate was the opening of the Gates of Paris during the third act of La Boheme. Said gates were hung on a scenery wall but someone had forgotten to fix the wall to the stage. As the gates were opening the wall began to fall and a soldier had to push it back upright and support it himself for the rest of the scene.

However Jim was never treated to the sight of Tosca trampolining as she committed suicide at the end of the opera, though maybe that is an operatic legend that has never actually happened.

Back to our twinners. Jim organised a coach trip for the members to Bristol Hippodrome to see Puccini's 'Turandot'. This went well and 'Encore' was heard.

Bad news always travels fast and sometimes good news gives it a good run for our money, so when other folk in his town learnt of this venture they asked if they too could come on the next trip, which of course they could.

Realising that there was money to be made for his favourite charity from his coach trips to Bristol, Jim expanded the programme to include ballets, musicals and the occasional play. The project grew like the proverbial Topsy' and by 2020 totalled over 260 trips and counting, although sadly the Covid pandemic has put a stop to Jim's theatre going at the time I am writing.

Not knowing how popular any one trip will be, Jim sets a price which covers, if twenty people book up, the cost of the tickets plus the coach hire, so when he fills a fifty-three seater coach a large profit is made which to date totals over £66 000, all of which is donated to charity, usually of course to the Red Cross.

Jim tells me that he loves this activity and is eager for it to start up again. All from Stephanie suggesting that he went to an inaugural twinning meeting. As I said, sometimes life takes off in surprising and unintentional directions.

The coach trips have generally passed off without incidents

though with Jim in charge there had to be some problems so here is an assortment.

The coach picks up in different towns along the route and in the early days Jim was not as careful as he needed to be with who was getting on where, and exactly where they should wait. Two friends were going together but they lived in different towns. On arriving at the third of their pick-up points where one of the friends was waiting she asked why her companion was not already on board.

Oh dear!

Jim decided that he had no choice but to go back to pick her up but when he got back there was no sign of her. On contacting her the next day with a grovel and a refund it turned out that she was waiting in the wrong place and, when the coach drove past her without stopping, she had gone back home, no doubt somewhat cross.

The extra time spent returning and then looking for the missing passenger led to the coach reaching the theatre with just seconds to spare.

Another lesson learnt.

As the years went by more and more people were carrying mobile phones with them and Jim now travels with everyone's mobile number so that he can phone them if they are not waiting where they are expected to be. He also is very precise about the actual picking up point.

On another trip they were on their way home late in the evening when a call came up the coach that a passenger was in trouble. The driver stopped the vehicle and Jim went to investigate, finding a passenger unconscious in their seat though fortunately still breathing.

An ambulance was summoned and the crew decided the unconscious casualty needed to be taken to hospital on a stretcher. How do you get a stretcher out of a coach? When you think about it the answer is: not easily.

As they were on a fairly narrow road with a thick hedge on their left the next step was to stop a lorry and a van to block the road. Then the coach was moved to the 'wrong' side so that the stretcher could be taken out of the passenger door. The happy ending is that the casualty made a full recovery.

Another time, again late in the evening as they rarely got away from Bristol before 10:30, the driver had started to pull away when a passenger called out that the luggage doors on the off-side were open. The driver did a rapid stop and started pressing switches on his dashboard, trying every knob in sight and some several times each. He knew that he had not opened the luggage doors himself but equally knew that the coach could not continue with them open. He got out and tried brute force but the doors were not having any of it. All that he could do was phone his company and get a replacement coach sent up for them, which took a couple of hours.

They had stopped outside a hotel and the manager kindly let the passengers wait in his lounge bar where they had an unplanned party.

When the replacement coach arrived it came with an engineer on board. He clambered into the luggage department and soon found the problem – a blown fuse. I guess it makes sense that if a fuse blows then the doors open themselves, rather than stay shut and so block access to the fuses.

By the time all the passengers had been persuaded that their party was over and they had seated themselves in the replacement coach the faulty one was fully operational again and they proceeded home in convoy.

Apollo Thirteen this was not, no slingshot round the moon was needed, and maybe the extra excitement added to making it a memorable trip for the theatre-goers, although it was well into the small hours by the time they got back to their homes.

The final story Jim has to tell of theatre-trip adventures was down to his failure to notice that he had booked tickets for a performance on the evening when the Glastonbury Festival patrons were accessing their site. Several miles from the turning into the Worthy Farm field the coach had to stop behind a huge line of stationary cars and assorted vans. The entry system has improved in recent years but this was before changes were made and the queue was very slow moving, veering on stationary. It looked as if they were going to be more than a little late getting to Bristol.

Fortunately a police motorcyclist came along towards the coach and the driver flagged him down, explaining that his destination was the Bristol Hippodrome theatre, not Michael Eavis's highly popular festival.

"Follow me!" said the policeman.

The coach pulled onto the wrong side of the road and drove past the waiting vehicles as if it was on the Champs Elysees until they reached the head of the queue at which point the police escort left them.

As you can probably imagine there was an equally big queue waiting on the Bristol side of the entrance. Jim's side of the road was of course clear, though any driver doing what they had just done would have met them head on. But all was well and they made the theatre before curtain up.

CHAPTER THIRTY-THREE

A Life Well Lived

My narrative is going to leave behind, for now, Jim's many jams and instead tell you of Stephanie's life with Jim.

Their home was built in 1907 on land that had been apple orchards and in their garden was a cooker apple that could well have been there from those far off days. It never fails to put on a terrific display of blossom in the spring followed by an impressive number of large cooker apples in the autumn.

Stephanie put her pharmaceutical skills to good use making many gallons of excellent apple wine. She was never sure of the proof rating of her brew although it certainly induced a warm glow after consumption of a glass.

Her skills and the uncertain effect of drinking her potion reminded Jim of his Victorian born Great Aunt Eliza who had vowed never to touch alcohol, although she was quite happy to drink the home-made parsnip wine made annually by Jim's uncle.

'Quite happy' probably describes correctly how Great Aunt Eliza felt after a couple of glasses of this seemingly innocuous brew but with no Proof rating on the label it couldn't be alcoholic could it; could it?!

In spite of my opening sentence to this chapter, Jim, reading the above, has again butted in to tell us of yet another of his brushes with fate. It involves the said tree, which he used to climb into for an annual winter pruning.

The last time that he did this he achieved his goal and thus had many branches and shoots on the ground under the tree. Bending down to pick one of them up he managed to bang his forehead on the trunk. It did not seem a severe injury, just painful and a lump. There was no blood and it was soon forgotten about.

However, you knew there had to be a however, some months later he realised that his roses no longer had their accustomed scent and that he, as he likes to put it, 'no longer smells'.

Various investigations at the hospital confirmed that he had indeed lost his olfactory ability. He knew that anyway but, as scans and tests revealed no clinical cause, the doctor insisted that Jim must have suffered a severe blow to his head. He denied this but later remembered his encounter with the apple tree and thinks that this must have been the cause.

I guess if one has to lose any of our five senses maybe the ability to enjoy the fragrance of a lovely rose is the least undesirable but Jim does have to be very careful with the gas stove.

And apple trees!

'OK Jim, can I continue to tell my reader about Stephanie please? Thanks.'

One autumn day Jim was called from his classroom as Stephanie had phoned school in a panic. She had had an accident and needed Jim at home urgently.

Wondering what on earth she had done to herself Jim found a teacher willing to sit with his class and tore off home.

There he found Stephanie in tears. Whilst preparing for her annual wine-making she had dropped a heavy glass demi-john and cracked the plastic sink. Hardly a major emergency and Jim, having calmed his wife down, was able to return to his class. The sink was soon replaced and the wine was as usual very drinkable.

Wine making was only a small part of how Stephanie filled her days. She enjoyed craft-work and joined a group to learn how to make 'Pergamano' greeting cards using cut out parchment paper and paints. She made many beautiful ones over the years as she and her sister both had considerable artistic talents.

She also loved labelling anything that kept still long enough. Nearly every box, drawer, container, ruler, pencil, pen, and hook bore either the details of its official use or that it was the property of either Stephanie or of Jim. This probably was as a result of her many years in the pharmacy where unlabelled jars and containers would be potentially highly dangerous and were very much a no-no.

Other hobbies included researching her family history, spurred on no doubt by the lure of the family fortune 'in chancery' awaiting a claimant. However, like her Lancashire relation who started this fanciful notion, Stephanie failed to find any positive connection with the wealthy Charnocks but she enjoyed the search and made several new friends along the way.

She had always enjoyed singing so she joined a local choir and sang as a soprano in many concerts. She became a u3a member and attended a group that sang folk songs and items from popular musicals under the title 'Singing For Fun'. Another u3a activity was the 'Music Appreciation' group to whom she lectured several times on the subject of Rachmaninoff's works.

I guess as a result of the philosophy 'If you can't beat them join them' she volunteered alongside Jim in the Red Cross, training as a first-aider so that she was able to join Jim on duties at local events which he much appreciated.

The list of her activities is impressive isn't it and I still haven't reached the end.

When Jim's daughter was working in Spain his wife went to evening school and learnt Spanish. Then as her hearing deteriorated with age she also attended lip reading classes.

For a few years she took a great interest in Astrology and she produced complex astrological charts for all the family who knew their important birth details; time, date and place. The charts produced revealed what talents they had yet to discover and what the future might hold for them, or not. At least they would then know what character they had and who they were most likely to get on well with, if they had not worked this out for themselves without the influence of heavenly bodies or at least not celestial ones.

Jim being Cancer and Stephanie being Pisces it was good news that astrology predicted that they would get on well together, which at least was true. However Jim does not feel that she believed all that seriously in the course of our lives being affected by where the planets are at any particular time.

Finally I must mention her many years of service for the local Talking Newspaper. These volunteers produced a monthly magazine on tapes that were posted out to members of the public with a problem with their sight. Much to Stephanie's delight one of the readers who joined her was Peter Goodwright, the radio and television impersonator and comedian, who had retired to her town. He had a lovely voice when reading on the tape.

Stephanie always liked being with people of note and was good at noticing famous faces in a crowd. Whilst with Jim she spotted, and chatted briefly to, Miriam Gargoyles in a lift, Ralph Fiennes in a theatre Foyer, Maggie Smith on a Bath street (though not in a van) and in a restaurant Paul McGann, who a good few years before had spent some months filming in their town. Others she conversed with when they came to give talks in the area were Lenny Henry, who grew up in her Midland town, and Alan Titchmarsh.

As you already know Stephanie held a candle, or two, for her conductor neighbour. She always went to his local concerts and made sure that she spoke to him, although she failed to receive any more kisses, on her cheeks or anywhere else.

Where was I? Oh yes, the Talking Newspaper. It will be no surprise to you that she became deeply involved with the project and for many years was their secretary, organising the various readers and recording teams for the weekly news tape and keeping minutes of their meetings.

◆ ◆ ◆

Stephanie was always able to make Jim laugh, surely a sign of a good marriage.

One source of amusement was their frequent deliberate use of Malapropisms. Favourites included fetching their perspirations from the chemist and taking part in many erections over the years, usually voting for Paddy Ashdown who Jim had walked with on a demo in Taunton and who was yet another man Stephanie fancied; she was not alone in that I am sure.

They (Jim and Stephanie, not her and Paddy, or not as far as Jim knows) always enjoyed a packet of crips on a Saturday evening while they watched Casuality. Enough of this nonsense!

Stephanie also had many catch phrases. She used to come naked out of the bathroom in the mornings with the announcement 'Nice clean white girl' or sometimes 'Bathroom Free Now', followed, after dressing and the painstaking application of her make-up, with 'Breakfast's Served Now.' When the cat refused to come in at night she was 'A Dirty Stop Out.' Then there was 'This is only ever a temporary situation.' when she was experiencing something that she wished that she was not experiencing. 'Don't force it Phoebe!' was also popular; this expression is known to other folk though no one seems to know for sure where it comes from.

Her instruction to Jim to 'Please put that away' is probably best not explained.

Later in their life, with both experiencing hearing loss, Stephanie invested in a railway guard's whistle which she used to blow to attract Jim's attention when he was in another room or in the garden, rather on the lines of Captain Von Trapp in 'The Sound of Music'.

One evening Stephanie watched a television documentary of the life of Agatha Christie where she discovered that Agatha and she had both qualified as pharmaceutical dispensers, taking their final examinations at the Apothecary's Hall, one of the Livery Halls in London. Both Stephanie and Agatha failed the practical part of their exam at their first attempt. Both passed the second time around. Stephanie thus found common ground with Agatha and no doubt if Agatha had still been alive she would have made a bee-line for her to talk about their shared experience.

With Agatha having 'gone before', Stephanie took as a consolation prize several visits to the annual Guilds of London Open Day. Displayed in The Apothecaries' Hall was Agatha's certificate and the volunteers on duty also managed to find Stephanie's entry in the Apothecaries' Examination Record Book.

Not to be outdone Stephanie had her own large ornate certificate framed and proudly displayed it on the landing of her house. She also went with Jim to visit Agatha's summer retreat in Devon where Jim was allowed to play her piano; this impressed Stephanie no end. As a final act of devotion to her fellow professional Stephanie ploughed through the vast majority of Agatha's books.

Fortunately for Jim this did not give her any murderous intentions towards him or anyone else.

CHAPTER THIRTY-FOUR

Until We Meet Again

In her early seventies Stephanie woke one morning not feeling too good, or as she often used to say in her best Lancashire accent, "I don't feel so well."

This time it was serious and Jim suspected that she was having a stroke although she showed no symptoms to fit the first three of the standard first aider's mantra of FAST (Face, Arms, Speech, Telephone). At least the last of these was acted on, an ambulance was summoned, and she was taken into hospital. By the next day Stephanie was completely paralysed on her right side.

This type of trauma is defined as an 'Evolving Stroke' which, as the name implies, comes on gradually with a slowly increasing cut off in the brain's blood supply rather than the typical symptoms of a sudden arterial blockage.

Stephanie was determined to overcome her disability and the next day, finding that she could not use her right hand to write, got Jim to bring her in a typewriter so that she could type letters to her friends using her left hand.

This was followed up during the next four weeks by demands for so many other items to be brought in that the nurses needed to install some extra cupboard space for her.

Jim's and Stephanie's twentieth wedding anniversary came whilst Stephanie was in hospital. Knowing that their ages when they married meant that a Golden Wedding anniversary was very unlikely they had instead celebrated fifty weeks of married bliss at an upmarket restaurant.

They had now made twenty in years so her sister, Jane, came to visit and the three had a celebratory lunch in the hospital restaurant where Jane invented a new sauce for roast beef.

For some reason that no doubt made sense to the staff, next to the help yourself vegetables was a jug which Jane assumed was gravy.

It wasn't.

Pouring custard onto roast beef is a novel, if not cordon bleu, idea but the chef decided that this was probably not some strange Birmingham custom and replaced her meal without any fuss.

After a month Jim was able to bring his wife home where she showed great determination to recover her normal functions and rewire her brain so that she would be able to walk and write again.

Within a year she was pretty much able to return to her previous busy life-style, including several holidays abroad. She made two trips with cousins, one back to Canada on the Rocky Mountaineer train and one on the new Queen Elizabeth liner, though this did not involve leaving the English Channel.

She went on her own to Dresden to see where Rachmaninoff had lived, although the British had seen to it that the residence was no longer there and, unlike much of the city, his lodgings had not been rebuilt after the war. However our Rachmaninoff groupie seemed happy enough to have seen where it used to be.

She also made several trips using National Express and the local buses to concerts in Birmingham where she was able to meet up with her sister to whom she was very close.

With a wayward right-hand side though she was no longer a safe driver and after a couple of scares accepted that she would have to rely on Jim and on public transport. She was still able to help him on long journeys by giving him route instructions, disdaining a satnav and much preferring a printed map which, as ever, she turned round when their journey involved heading towards the bottom of the page.

◆ ◆ ◆

As I said, Stephanie made a great recovery and celebrated her eightieth birthday in style.

Shortly after this though she began to suffer from deep depression. Her state of mind was further worsened when she received the utterly unexpected news of the sudden death of her apparently robustly healthy sister who for years past she had chattered to on the phone several times a week.

Churchill's 'black dog' was nothing new to her but this time, perhaps exacerbated by the damage the stroke had done to her brain, she did not fully get over it and so Jim became her carer.

In 2019 along came the news of the new variety of Corona viruses, later specifically named as Covid 19, which eventually affected the whole world and caused a huge number of deaths.

Once the virus started mutating, and not wishing to seem to be blaming any one country of origin for it having first appeared in their country, the authorities started instructing the population in the Greek alphabet, though I am not sure if the Greeks were asked if this was OK with them. At the time of writing we have fifteen named ones, from Alpha through to Lambda. I guess that will now be well out of date given the ease with which the virus mutates and by the time you read this they could well have run out of Greek letters. Perhaps they will use Chinese characters which have several thousand variations.

That should do it shouldn't it?

With restaurants shut down and visits to friends and relations not allowed, Stephanie spent her days reading and watching the television, often with Poppy, their attack cat, on her lap

Poppy was a 'rescued' tortoiseshell cat and what she had suffered in her past they did not know. It had certainly left her very defensive. She was usually OK to stroke if one kept ones hand behind her eye-line but get a hand in front of her and she pounced. Stephanie, Jim and several bloodied visitors soon found this out to their cost.

Then on a visit to the vet because she was losing weight Poppy was diagnosed with a heart murmur and an over active thyroid so, what with medication and regular blood tests, she ended up being very expensive.

Another of Stephanie's expressions was "I may be expensive but I'm worth it." and Jim and Stephanie agreed that this applied to Poppy as well.

I haven't exhausted Stephanie's expression store. Yet another, which proved eventually all too apt, was "Don't have another fall dearie!".

One evening while coming to bed Stephanie shrieked

"Oh no!"

as she lost her balance whilst passing the top of the carpeted stairs and tumbled all the way to the bottom.

Her guardian angel must have been on point-duty as the only damage she did was bruises and a strained knee.

A few weeks later though she again lost the use of her right leg and was admitted to hospital where a second evolving stroke was diagnosed.

With Covid precautions in place this was not a good time to be in hospital, if there is ever a good time, so that visiting was very restricted but Jim managed to book in most days for a half-hour slot. Stephanie was very disabled, unable to swallow, speak, write or stand. With her hearing disability and masks making lip-reading impossible Jim could only communicate with her by writing on a pad what he wanted to say.

It was hard.

Their thirtieth wedding anniversary came, like their twentieth, whilst Stephanie was in hospital but they managed to observe their anniversary together.

Stephanie's condition stabilised enough for her to be discharged to a care home, all the medics concerned agreeing that Jim would not be able to provide at home the twenty-four hour care she now needed. This Stephanie found hard to accept but no doubt she hoped it was, again with one of her catch phrases, 'only ever a temporary situation'.

A temporary situation it indeed turned out to be as, after less than two months in the care home, Stephanie had another fall and some days later her condition deteriorated.

She was taken into hospital and Jim was told on the phone by the hospital doctor that she had suffered a severe bleed on her brain, that she was unconscious, and that a recovery was very unlikely. Knowing how disabled Stephanie already was, the decision was taken to let her depart in peace.

She managed one final co-incidence, or more accurately double coincidence, of which she was sadly unaware.

She had in Lancashire a cousin, Jean, who she was very fond of and felt especially close to as they shared the same birth date, though several years apart.

Jean had gone into hospital a few years before for a replacement knee operation. Although this went well she was in much pain afterwards and a locum doctor prescribed a strong analgesic without seemingly being aware of Jean's existing bronchial condition for which the drug was contra-indicated. The drug suppressed her breathing which escaped the attention of the nursing staff who thought she was in a deep sleep and she passed away.

This had led to an inquest which Jim and Stephanie had attended, though somewhat surprisingly the prescribing doctor did not. A narrative verdict was the outcome and as in The Lion and Albert it seemed that 'no one was really to blame'.

It was now Stephanie's turn for an inquest as the hospital doctor was concerned about the bruising on Stephanie's front.

Not only had Stephanie and Jean shared the same birthday but both had died on the same date and both deaths had resulted in an inquest. A final huge coincidence.

The coroner at Stephanie's established that Stephanie had fallen in her care-home room a fortnight before and had hit her head. This must have weakened an artery which led to the bleed in her brain, so his verdict was 'Accidental Death'.

The last time Jim saw his wife was in her care home before fresh Covid concerns stopped visiting. They were not allowed to touch each other but she had been practising her speech and managed to say "I love you." and had blown him a kiss. This memory has consoled him in his loss.

Stephanie as usual found a way to have the last word in an argument.

One very minor disagreement over the years had been where to hang their fairly heavy peg-bag. Jim wanted it on a strong hook on the wall whereas Stephanie wanted it on a fairly flimsy door which Jim was worried would warp under the strain.

Some weeks after his wife's death he noticed that, in her 'everything must be labelled' obsession which we have already visited, she had stuck a label 'Hook for Peg Bag' above her preferred site on the flimsy door!

No wonder he loved her so much.

CHAPTER THIRTY-FIVE

Looking Back

Having been his wife's carer for a couple of years, Jim finding himself alone and sole 'cook and bottle washer' was not such a shock as it could have been. His sister and Helen, his daughter, were very supportive, both phoning him every day.

You may remember his first daughter was comforted in her last days by an 'angel cat' and Jim too has been helped in his loneliness by another feline companion.

Poppy, the 'attack cat' died of old age a few weeks before Stephanie herself passed away and Helen thought that another cat should be found to give her dad some company. Searching the internet a disabled rescue cat was found and they named her 'Belle'.

The cattery was pleased to have found someone prepared to give a disabled cat a home but they warned Jim that she would probably take some days to settle in at her new home.

This proved far from true.

Within five minutes of arriving at Jim's home she leapt up onto his lap and purred liked a steam-engine.

Her affection has not waned! She is yet another one deserving of the title 'Angel Cat'. Do I detect a title for another book there?

For now though it is time to leave Jim to get on with his new life as a widower, but not before I ask him how he would sum up his life.

He thinks the General Confession does that for us:

Almighty and most merciful Father,
We have erred and strayed from thy ways like lost sheep,
We have followed too much
The devices and desires of our own hearts,
We have offended against thy holy laws,
We have left undone those things
Which we ought to have done,
And we have done those things
Which we ought not to have done;
And there is no health in us.
But thou, O Lord, have mercy upon us, miserable offenders.
Spare thou them, O God, which confess their faults.
Restore thou them that are penitent;
According to thy promises declared unto mankind
In Christ Jesu our Lord.
And grant, O most merciful Father, for His sake,
That we may hereafter
Live a godly, righteous, and sober life,
To the glory of thy holy Name. Amen.

Jim thinks that covers just about everything and he is sure he will at least have no trouble with the 'sober' bit.

He feels that he always did his best to help his companions, be they soulmates, friends, or strangers, as they made their way through life together.

He hopes to be able to continue to be of use to others for the precious time he has left.

Whatever life has thrown at Jim, whatever its ups and downs, looking back he has enjoyed it and wouldn't have missed it for the world!

Let's give Stephanie what she usually got, the last word.

As she used to say:

"Things always look better on reflection."

◆ ◆ ◆

About The Author

Christopher Cox is a retired teacher and author of a popular mathematics text book series. He is now a Red Cross volunteer, just like Jim!

All profits from sales of this book will be donated to The British Red Cross to support Langport Centre Shop.

Books By This Author

'Total Experience Corner - A Year in Jamaica' is a memoire of a year teaching in the Jamaican bush. Also published on Amazon it is both highly amusing and heart-breaking. A bit like this one.

Thank You

The author warmly thanks his sister, Marion, for filling in some of the gaps in Jim's ancestry, his daughter for some much needed editing, and his friend Suzanne for her encouragement.

Also he thanks you for supporting his beloved Red Cross by purchasing this book.

Printed in Great Britain
by Amazon

70216652R00108